# CONGREGATIONS
# IN
# CHANGE

*A Project Test Pattern Book*
*in Parish Development*

# CONGREGATIONS
## IN
## CHANGE

*Elisa L. DesPortes*

*Foreword by Cynthia C. Wedel*
*Preface by Loren B. Mead*

*A Crossroad Book*
THE SEABURY PRESS · NEW YORK

2-6-74

*Congregations in Change* is published under the auspices of the
National Advisory Committee on Evangelism, the Rt. Rev. Lloyd Gressle,
Chairman, and the Executive Council of the Episcopal Church.

Copyright © 1973 by Project Test Pattern
Library of Congress Catalog Card Number: 73–77768
ISBN: 0–8164–2085–8
Text and cover design by Carol Basen
Cover design adapted from a silk screen painting
by Lou Stovall and Walter Hopps, February, 1971.
Printed in the United States of America

## FOREWORD

The greatest problem facing every institution in today's society—including the Church—is the problem of change. The world is changing, society is changing, people are changing. Yet institutions, by their very nature, tend to resist change. Even an institution which may have come into being as an agent of change soon develops its own structures, relationships, and ways of working which it will—consciously or unconsciously—fight to preserve.

The Church, as an institution with very long traditions, faces real problems in a changing world. This can be clearly seen in the crises confronting the Church at all levels—on the local level where membership and funds may be lessening while tension and alienation increase, and on the national level which finds itself under growing attacks from its constituency. There are two basic patterns which indicate that a parish church may be heading for trouble. One is a situation where change is apparent—such as a changing neighborhood, decreasing attendance, financial problems, or the growth of antagonistic factions. The other and potentially more dangerous situation is where problems are not apparent, things seem to be moving along as they always have, and the church is unaffected by changes going on around it. In the latter case, it is possible that there really is no problem. The church may actually be effective and successful. But it is not often safe to assume this without an occasional assessment of needs and performance.

In a very real sense, the health of the whole Church depends upon vital, live local congregations. Yet it is at the level of the local congregation that people have their deepest loyalties and the greatest resistance to change. The intimate relationship between pastor and people makes it difficult for either to criticize the other, or to raise questions which might seem to imply criticism. The temptation is to "let sleeping dogs lie," to hope that whatever suggests change or a need for change will go away if no one makes an issue of it. For this reason a great many congregations are on the verge of very serious trouble, which will eventually cause problems throughout the entire Church.

It was awareness of the critical need for change and renewal of congregations which led to the development of Project Test Pattern. Through its program many parishes have been helped to face the need for change and enter into a process of renewal. Many things distinguish Project Test Pattern from the usual church program for renewal. There is no standard plan to be followed, nor a predetermined result. Each parish is seen for what it is—a unique combination of circumstances, personalities, problems, and opportunities. The only constant feature of the PTP operation is the introduction of an outside consultant to work with the parish and to help pastor and people discover and solve their own problems.

At least until the present time, PTP has not attempted

books which generalize its findings or present a plan for change or renewal. Instead, Elisa DesPortes has written case studies as in the earlier *New Hope for Congregations* by Loren Mead, and this book. To me this indicates their recognition of the futility of trying to provide what many people ask for: a book or manual which will outline how to bring about renewal or change. A thoughtful reading of either of the PTP publications indicates certain recurring patterns. The relationship between pastor and people is often a problem, even when there is no antagonism. In several of the cases studied in this volume, the tendency of the minister to make all the decisions and to carry all the burdens is matched by the passivity and lack of involvement of the members of the parish. The lack of any clear goals for the parish is another persistent problem, as is an ever-present trend to misjudge and fail to sense the hopes, desires, and antipathies of many members. Poor communication within the congregation and with those outside is often an element. In at least one case, the influence of community patterns and norms of behavior was a critical factor in the difficulties a church faced.

Reading these detailed and honest accounts of what happened when a parish decided to take the chance of examining itself will bring many "aha! aha!" moments—things the reader has experienced in one church or another. There are no panaceas or easy answers, but various processes begin to make sense. The usefulness of the outside consultant as catalyst is apparent. The need for accurate information about facts *and* feelings becomes clear. Above all, there is the obvious requirement that as many of the congregation as possible be involved in and committed to the process.

Anyone looking for an easy solution to the malaise of

their church will be disappointed in this book. But those who know that the local congregation is extremely important and worth a lot of pain and hard work will find here the seeds of real hope and many clues to the process of renewal.

*Cynthia C. Wedel*

# PREFACE

Elisa DesPortes, who for three years has been studying the dynamics of change in local congregations, has brought together here the stories of a remarkable group of congregations.

They are remarkable, not for any of the externals by which congregations are normally judged, but for their willingness to take the risks of growing and changing. Their people are ordinary Christian folk, not "saints"— but they are acting on convictions that are often given only lip service elsewhere.

Their clergy, for example, are trying to learn how to step out from behind traditional structures and roles and lead as participants and collaborators with their laity. The process is becoming a major educational intervention in their lives, and is both painful and joyful in turn. It takes courage and willingness to face the anxiety of risk.

Their laity, too, share the risks of learning new patterns of life in their congregations. They tend, in their stories, to take more responsibility and leadership in the works of mission and nurture in their congregation.

Each person in these stories is conscious of trying out new patterns of congregational life. All have been willing to do so because of their unique understanding of their relationship to Jesus Christ and their relationship to others, both inside and outside the Church. A symbol of their commitment is their willingness to share their experience without resorting to pseudonyms.

Elisa DesPortes, then, is letting us see how a new kind of Church is being born; a church in which role is determined by the mission task, not by prestige; a church where "ministry" describes what happens; a church that has enough Christian faith to step out on new paths, to take risks, and even to make mistakes; a church willing to learn from its experience and to share its experience openly so that others might learn.

These congregations have been operating as centers for learning, experiencing, and sharing the truths of the faith. As such, they give me hope that many congregations may become similar centers, supporting and strengthening Christians for their tasks in the world. In essence, the stories of these congregations encourage me in my dream that any congregation—yours, for example—can be a center of theological education, of mission action, of personal growth, of faith-strategy, and a center where the hopes and fears of the community and the world are celebrated and faced each week.

Elisa has given a lot of herself to this book and these stories. As one of the central-core staff of Project Test Pattern for three years, she participated in the shaping of that temporary action-research agency, with major responsibility for developing stories from the research data developed by our network of parish development advisers. Three chapters of the earlier PTP book, *New Hope for Congregations* by Loren B. Mead (New York: Seabury

Press, 1972)* were researched and written by Elisa DesPortes.

In *Congregations in Change* she makes a major contribution to our ability to understand and improve the work of parish development.

*Loren B. Mead*
LENT, 1973

* This book is one of a list of resources available from Project Test Pattern, Mt. St. Alban, Washington, D.C. 20016.

# AUTHOR'S NOTE

*Congregations in Change* is an attempt to make the learnings of Project Test Pattern available to the Church at
large. The six case histories in this book are written as a
companion volume to *New Hope for Congregations,* Project Test Pattern's first book, by Loren B. Mead, director.
Although the congregations and consultations in both
books are similar, *Congregations in Change* tells these
parish stories with more detail and greater depth. They
are aimed at a reader who is already familiar with the
ideas and stories in *New Hope for Congregations.*

Each story evolved from a rather complex set of docu-
ments and research material. With the exception of All
Souls' Church, Richmond, each church has participated in
a Project Test Pattern consultation. The consultant team
sent to the PTP headquarters in Washington, D.C., a detailed report of every contact with the client parish. Note-
books were kept on every consultation and included such
things as the weekly parish bulletin and newsletter, car-
bons of all correspondence and in-depth write-ups of consultant visits. These valuable reports included events, de-

signs, and personal reflections, along with raw data from congregational meetings, interviews, and conferences.

After the consultation had been completed, a team of interviewers spent several days in the parish to gather more information. Interviews were conducted with the consultants, the rector, and his staff. The research team also talked with different types of parishioners ranging from very active, involved leaders to inactive fringe people. PTP interviewers talked with people who were very much in favor of the consultation as well as with people who were against it. Young people were interviewed as well as community or neighborhood leaders who were not church members. After all the different perspectives had been noted, these six case histories were written.

The primary purpose of this book is to describe the change process in specific churches. Central focus is given to the experience of consultation, though much was learned about other aspects of parish life. Several guidelines were used to select these cases. PTP selected churches with a variety of settings—urban, inner city, suburban, and rural. Towns were large, middle-sized, and small. An effort was made to get a wide geographical spread, though this was obviously not a primary consideration. Racial and socio-economic differences were also a consideration. From a more technical perspective, PTP developed the cases which, from our raw data, indicated the greatest learnings in terms of both consultation and parish life.

Both parishioners and consultants chose to have their real names used in the book. Project Test Pattern preferred to use the original names and places in order to maintain a norm of openness.

More important, each parish and each person in this book is still living. Their stories do not end with the conclusions of each chapter. In many ways PTP observed only a portion of each parish's life, and that life is by no means over. By the time *Congregations in Change* is published, life will be very different in each place.

No one person produced *Congregations in Change*. Many people gave of their talent, time, and energy to make this book possible. First are the consultants who provided PTP with the basic written material. The next step involved the skilled people who visited each parish to conduct interviews. My many thanks go to those who traveled with me: the Rev. William Paran, for his help in Chicago; the Rev. William Dols in Washington; the Rev. Kyle McGee in Richmond; and the Rev. Dr. Umhau Wolf in Texarkana. I am grateful to Loren Mead and Don Morse for their field trip to Birmingham.

After all the information had been gathered back in Washington, D.C., PTP's core staff really went to work. Loren Mead, director of PTP, continually encouraged me to write this book. He personally assumed my administrative responsibilities and single-handedly kept the wheels of PTP going, freeing me to concentrate on the research and writing. Loren also served as my adviser and editor. I particularly appreciate his remarkable sensitivity and his ability to express difficult experiences objectively and to communicate care and honor. I've learned a lot from him.

Throughout the entire time of compiling this book, there were two people who continually worked to produce the final manuscript. A special appreciation goes to Mrs. Wilma Swanson and Mrs. Katey Harris Meares for their technical skill. These two friends typed and retyped volumes of interviews, notes, and drafts. Both of them gave me the day-to-day personal support that I needed. A simple "thank you" does not seem enough.

Besides PTP's full-time staff, Mrs. Celia Hahn made a

major contribution to *Congregations in Change*. Celia is both the author of the chapter on the Church of the Transfiguration and the editor of the entire work. I valued Celia's talent and her tact at every point along the way. Her literary skill is enhanced by her ability to give feedback in such a manner that I could hear it and still want to try a rewrite "one more time."

Mrs. Margaret Brown in Washington, D.C., deserves praise and thanks for her drawings of each parish.

Another thank you goes to Bob Gilday, the editor at the Seabury Press, whose delightful sense of humor and casual manner put me at ease. All of these people have made *Congregations in Change* possible.

In many ways I feel that each parish in this book became my own parish. We went through a lot together. Sometimes our relationship was joyous and at other times we lived through a lot of pain and hard times. Because of the openness and honesty of the parishioners, it was easy for me to share their pride and their anxiety. This book is, therefore, a product of more than one person. This book belongs to the people whose experiences are related in it. Their great contribution was their willingness to let me intrude into their thoughts, experiences, and feelings. The stories are their stories. The words and learnings are their words and learnings, given generously and in simple faith that the gift would be used justly and that it might have some meaning.

To them I dedicate this book.

E. L. D.

# CONTENTS

# CONGREGATIONS
## IN
## CHANGE

# 1

## THE STORY OF ST. PAUL AND
## THE REDEEMER

THE NEIGHBORHOOD

For an outsider the simplest way to understand The Church of St. Paul and The Redeemer is to take a ride through its neighborhood and surrounding communities. Located on the South Side of Chicago, at Dorchester and Forty-ninth Streets, the Episcopal Church of St. Paul and The Redeemer is firmly planted in a fifteen-block area called Hyde Park-Kenwood. Hyde Park-Kenwood, a middle-class neighborhood, surrounds the University of Chicago and these two in turn are surrounded on three sides by the South Side ghetto—the largest ghetto in the United States west of Bedford-Stuyvesant. Most parishioners of St. Paul and The Redeemer live in Hyde Park-Kenwood and are strongly influenced by the physical, economic, and social forces around them.

Residents of Hyde Park-Kenwood speak intensely about their neighborhood and describe it with a very pronounced sense of community. Some consider it one of the few stable urban communities in the country—perhaps the only one in the past quarter of a century to survive the onslaught of the ghetto and emerge as a cohesive, integrated whole. The residents claim that their neighborhood is not filled with racial tension, but is, rather, a middle-class island where people of both races live by choice, even though it is surrounded by substandard black housing.

The people living in Hyde Park-Kenwood are prosperous blacks and whites, and there is very little public housing. As one resident put it: "If people have enough money to buy a home in Hyde Park-Kenwood, then we do not worry about race or the quality of the neighborhood." The blacks are established, prominent, affluent professionals. The whites are self-consciously liberal professionals. Another description of Hyde Park-Kenwood sums it up as "the great liberal community where blacks and whites stand together against the lower class."

Hyde Park-Kenwood is a community with very deep buffer zones to keep the poor out and prevent deterioration. Over the years, the people have battled to maintain an integrated, stable neighborhood and to protect their community from the slums. There are many one-way and dead-end streets which, according to one explanation, are a deliberate attempt to discourage the surrounding residents from driving through the area.

Hyde Park-Kenwood is also a company-owned town— the company being the University of Chicago, which owns half the land and employs half the working population. For the past twenty-five years the University of Chicago has been buying up the old buildings and building new ones in order to squeeze out the ghetto and save the university. Besides the homes where many of the faculty live, the area contains institutional buildings of the university, dormitories, and fraternity houses. Residents claim that the University of Chicago spends over one million dollars a year for private police protection for the neighborhood. Its campus begins one mile from the Church of St. Paul and The Redeemer.

Two blocks to the north of St. Paul and The Redeemer, on Forty-seventh Street, is North Kenwood, which stretches twelve blocks. North Kenwood is considered one of the most destitute areas of Chicago. It contains empty, deserted-shell housing along with some public housing, and is described as hard-core ghetto with serious drug and poverty problems. The fringe area between North Kenwood and Hyde Park-Kenwood contains vacant lots and rundown buildings—the kind that are being "urban renewed" out.

To the south of the church, at the end of Hyde Park-Kenwood, is a one-block wide, fairly deep expanse of green, which was once the Midway of the Columbian Exposition. In the winter, the sunken area is iced and used for sports. In the summer it is made into a park. The Midway divides the University of Chicago and Hyde Park-Kenwood from the poverty area of Woodlawn. Woodlawn, like North Kenwood, is one of the most destitute parts of the city. It has been called "post ghetto" because it is run-down and devastated from fires, abandoned buildings, and demolition. It has also been described as "Dresden after the war" because of these empty, blackened buildings. Population dropped 40 percent in the four years between 1966 and 1970, with public school attendance dropping 35 percent. In 1970 1,600 fires were reported in a square-mile area of Woodlawn. No arrests for arson were made. Nicholas von Hoffman, in his commentary in the *Washington Post*, described the burning this way: "The reasoning goes that since urban renewal had failed, housing rehabilitation had failed, public schools had failed, in short, all that this city has undertaken has failed, the best idea would be to let the blacks burn their way out into the suburbs so that the whites can come back and re-elect Mayor Daley forever."

Blacks began moving into Woodlawn around 1948. As a result Hyde Park-Kenwood organized and founded the Southeast Chicago Commission, strongly tied to the University of Chicago, and the Hyde Park-Kenwood Community Conference. These two organizations were created to save the neighborhood. The late Saul Alinsky, one of the first community organizers in the country, began with The Woodlawn Organization (TWO) to organize that community for jobs and better housing. In the sixties, Alinsky's organization frequently challenged the University of Chicago, sometimes with success.

About ten years ago a group of eight or ten black youths formed a block club in Woodlawn called the Blackstone Rangers. The club grew rapidly to 4,600 members and became the strongest gang on the South Side. Since they were located in Woodlawn and North Kenwood, Hyde Park-Kenwood became a corridor between the two black communities for the Blackstone Rangers. Since then, because most of their leaders, "the Main Twenty-one," are in jail or under indictment, the Rangers have become dispersed and disorganized. Some people believe that the fact that the area of Woodlawn has never had a riot is partially due to the Rangers, who are not interested in that kind of trouble.


THE PARISH

As part of this complex side of Chicago, the Church of St. Paul and The Redeemer reflects in its history and present life a diversity of forces. Physically it has a rather large church building with a connecting parish house containing offices and meeting rooms. The buildings and individual wings are locked at all times, and the local police recommend that when night meetings are held the blinds be drawn on the windows. On one occasion bullets were fired through a window, and there have been a number of break-ins and thefts. The custodian, when questioned about these attacks and precautions, said that it only reflected the atmosphere of the neighborhood and did not indicate any particular hostility toward the church. Parishioners see themselves as cautious but not frightened of the surrounding poor blacks, and they consider the actual presence of St. Paul and The Redeemer as more natural than unnatural to the neighborhood. One local minister in the area believes that St. Paul and The Redeemer is one of the few institutions that has seriously attempted to look at the neighborhood realistically.

There are 400 communicant members of St. Paul and The Redeemer, and average church attendance is around 170. The black constituency, 30 to 40 percent of the present congregation, but decreasing, is made up of prominent and often powerful people. Except for several acolytes and young girls and boys who come in from North Kenwood, there are few ghetto blacks.

As a corporate body, St. Paul and The Redeemer is not a socially active parish. On an individual basis, members are very active but, for the most part, prefer not to operate on a corporate parish level. In the past, members were heavily involved with social action through marches, sit-ins, and arrests, but as one member says, "The parish. is weary of this now." Another parishioner explained the position the church has developed:

This parish is actively committed *not* to minister to the ghetto. We make no point of going out into the surrounding areas. In the vestry two years ago we made a conscious decision against a social action ministry. Rather we decided to keep the parish together. We voted down every issue on the community.

Another active parishioner sees St. Paul and The Redeemer as having a very real sense of a church as a *religious place*, a place where the Holy Spirit can and does renew its members' life corporately as well as individually. "The very center of our church life is religion as a human experience larger than social action issues and social action forums on abortion and Christian action."

THE MERGER

The history of St. Paul and The Redeemer is similar to that of its neighborhood. It has been through many transition periods. The present congregation is the result of the merger of two local churches: St. Paul's and the Church of The Redeemer.

St. Paul's—a "low church," fifty percent white and fifty percent black—was once one of the wealthiest churches in the diocese and had a large endowment. In 1956 this great gothic stone church burned to the ground. The lost property was worth one-half million dollars. Priceless art treasures and magnificent stained glass windows were destroyed. The present church was built in 1958 with the support of the Diocese of Chicago.

The Church of The Redeemer was a younger, "high church" parish, made up mostly of white liberal professionals, many of whom were on the faculty of the University of Chicago, six blocks away. Approximately 10 to 15 percent of the congregation was black. Redeemer, realizing that it was spending most of its money to support the building, began in 1966 to look at ways to merge or combine with other local churches. It went through a lengthy process of search and negotiation, using methods of behavioral science to help prepare the congregation for the coming change. It approached several churches in the area but was turned down.

In late 1967 St. Paul's Church and the Church of The Redeemer decided to merge and form one congregation, St. Paul and The Redeemer. The Redeemer people moved over to the St. Paul's building, and the Rev. Warner C. White, rector of Redeemer, became rector of St. Paul and The Redeemer. The rector of St. Paul's, the Rev. Joseph Dickson, became associate rector of St. Paul and The Redeemer for an eighteen-month period.

There are many different versions of the merger story. Redeemer people see it one way, while St. Paul people see it another way, and various subgroups from each church see it yet another way. An official document stated how the merger was to be done, but today hardly any member remembers that document or its contents.

Though there is no general consensus on what happened or why, one fact is most evident and generally agreed on. The merger was a traumatic, difficult, and painful process. It produced suspicion, hostility, and division among groups on both sides. The feelings of the different groups are intense, personal, submerged, and unresolved. The conflict was in terms of both issues and personalities. There were many splits caused by the merger: St. Paul's vs. Redeemer, black vs. white, liberal vs. conservative, high church vs. low church, those loyal to Joe Dickson vs. those opposed to him, those who felt that Redeemer had taken over St. Paul's vs. those who saw St. Paul's as desperate and dying. The Rev. Al Moss, the black curate, who arrived shortly after the merger, described the conflict as follows: "The congregation was really broken and split into two groups that seemed to be pathologically demolishing each other —the blacks and the whites. Tension was so strong that many felt that the situation would blow any day."

The first years of the merger were chaotic and difficult. The present parish secretary, Ms. Cajsa Elo, describes their situation as follows: "We had double of everything—two rectors, two secretaries, two sextons, and two vestries. People were upset and confused. Division was everywhere."

Al Moss and Warner White attempted to bring some unity to the divisive factions by meeting with groups of parishioners in one of their homes to talk about the problems of the parish. Church attendance, although initially increasing, had now begun to drop. Their talks never resulted in any programs or any implementation of ideas, and the people felt frustrated. Blacks were outnumbered and often felt swamped by the intellectualism and sophistication of the whites. Moss saw his role as one of support for the rector and also as an articulator of the black feelings in the parish.

In the summer of 1968, six months into the merger, St. Paul and The Redeemer participated in a very controversial program for neighborhood youth. The Coordinated Youth Program (CYP) was sponsored by the YMCA and open to all youths. St. Paul and The Redeemer provided a building and volunteers, thinking that the local high school youth would participate. But, as Warner White later described the events of this period:

On the first night the Blackstone Rangers flooded in. That was also the time when hearings concerning the Rangers were going on in Washington. We held three emergency vestry meetings, I delayed my vacation, and we finally voted to go ahead. That fall we had several parish discussions on the matter. The bishop was present at one of them—at which time the Rangers staged a walk-in and a walk-out.

The program lasted a second summer. Finally, after intense community reaction against the CYP (the residential blacks strongly opposed it because their sons and daughters were being harassed by the gangs), the YMCA decided to end the program. Many parishioners were upset that St. Paul and The Redeemer had participated in the CYP. It proved to be particularly unsettling since the parish was still feeling the effects of the merger. As one parishioner put it: "We learned that you don't deal naively with the Blackstone Rangers."

EARLY PROBLEMS

That year, 1969, was a difficult year for St. Paul and The Redeemer in other ways. A new vestry was elected in the hope of providing fairer representation of the diverse elements within the parish. But the new members, although they tried to be very businesslike, found it difficult to communicate with each other, and a workshop was set up to help them. In the spring, the parish sponsored a Vietnam teach-in, which proved to be a divisive force and had to be dropped. By June, Joe Dickson, who had been a rather controversial figure, resigned as associate rector.

The following year things were more settled. The morale problem seemed to be improving, the parish was more unified and the people better able to work together. The vestry and rector were beginning to develop effective plans. As Warner White put it: "The train was on the track."

In Advent, a group of parishioners and Warner White began liturgical experimentation in an effort to develop a more satisfying worship service. They formed a liturgical committee and worked diligently to plan the liturgy and to change the interior of the nave and chancel. Pews were rearranged, bright banners and altar hangings were made, and the large wooden crucifix over the altar was polychromed. The parish, though not always flexible, began to experiment with Sunday morning worship, trying a variety of styles and liturgies. New people came, as well as students from the University of Chicago who had chosen St. Paul and The Redeemer as their church off campus. The atmosphere was decidedly more optimistic and unified. Explaining the changes, the rector said: "I saw the liturgical changes as the outward sign that we had succeeded in morale-building."

There were over a dozen nonparochial clergy who attended St. Paul and The Redeemer and Warner White used them extensively in preaching and celebrating the liturgy. The choirmaster and organist, a leading musician in the Chicago area, developed a strong choir—one of the best in Chicago. The congregation had a special interest in classical music and sang most of the service, using instrumental pieces to complement the liturgy. A large group of acolytes, both boys and girls, was also developed and became the youth group of the church. As one member described it:

The liturgy is so joyful. Everyone participates. That's our greatest strength. At the parish meeting in June 1971, we voted by a 90 percent majority in favor of the changes. Attendance has also risen. After the Sunday service we have a breakfast downstairs with coffee, rolls, and milk. It's a time for everyone to get together. A lot of new faces and even some old ones who had left are coming back because of the liturgy.

IN SEARCH OF A CONTRACT

In the Spring of 1970 the Rev. Marshall Megginson, a local clergyman in the Chicago area, and Mrs. Ann Rathbun, a human relations trainer and church professional, had been selected and briefly trained in parish consultation by Project Test Pattern.

Megginson and Rathbun were one of fifteen teams who were asked to work with a congregation to test out parish consultation. They asked the Bishop of Chicago to suggest parishes where they might work as parish consultants. The bishop wanted to use the consultants in critical situations where clergy and congregations were experiencing severe conflict. The consultants visited several parishes suggested by the bishop, but did not develop a contract. They felt that the conditions necessary for a long-term parish consultation were not present in these troubled spots, nor did the parishes show enough interest and commitment to sustain the kind of work the consultants wanted to do. After three unsuccessful attempts, Megginson and Rathbun decided that they would look for a parish that was fairly healthy, stable, and open to trying something new. They wanted one where the relationship between the rector and the congregation had not collapsed. At the same time, the consultants, having spent a lot of time on these other potential clients, were feeling pressured to get a contract with a church. One member of the team commented: "We felt pressured to sell a product because parishes were not coming to us for help."

Finally, Megginson and Rathbun decided to approach St. Paul and The Redeemer for a possible contract. Both consultants knew the rector and had worked with the vestry and several parish groups previously. They also felt the parish was open to growth and new possibilities. With the bishop's approval, they talked over their proposal with Warner White. White had also been trained in parish consultation and was immediately enthusiastic about using these former resource people in their new roles as parish consultants. He began to think of ways they could best present their proposal to the vestry. The team prepared a brief outline on Project Test Pattern, which the rector amended and distributed to the vestry. The consultants were then given an appointment to discuss their proposal at a vestry meeting on June 6, 1970.

At the meeting, the vestry's consideration of the PTP consultation was the third major issue on the agenda and

was scheduled for 11:00 P.M. The parish secretary and
clerk of the vestry, Cajsa Elo, described the situation as
follows:

The vestry at that time was operating under nearly impossible
agendas. The quantity of material it had to handle was far too
much to digest adequately. As the minutes say, PTP was scheduled at 11:00 P.M. The vestry was exhausted already. At the
time of this meeting, the vestry and rector were still operating under the old style of leadership, *i.e.*, with the rector
holding the entire authority bag, even though great strides had
already been made to begin changing that style. So, items like
PTP came in as projects the rector wanted to sell and the
vestry was persuaded to buy, which it usually did.

Megginson and Rathbun attended the vestry meeting to
answer any questions the members might have and also to
outline the initial steps of the consultation: getting an
overview of the parish to see more clearly the resources,
needs, and problems; and following this with action steps.
A liaison committee of the vestry would be set up to work
closely with the consultants.

The vestry responded with ambivalence about parish
consultation, and there were several opposing views. For
some members, the idea of an overview meant a questionnaire, and they had already been given too many
questionnaires in the past. Consultation also represented
a demand for more money and the parish was fighting for
a self-sustaining budget. The treasurer was against it,
while another vestryman hoped the parish would pay an
appropriate sum for the services. The consultants replied
that they recognized St. Paul and The Redeemer's financial problems, and were willing to compromise because
they needed a pilot project. Several vestrymen wondered
whether they were giving or receiving help. But some
welcomed a contract because they wanted to support a

project of the national church and thought the Hyde Park-Kenwood community was unique and therefore valuable to the research project.

On the more favorable side, there were possible advantages to St. Paul and The Redeemer. Consultation could help improve the church's ability to make decisions and carry them out. The parish could use help in serving the neighborhood. Perhaps consultation might help answer such questions as: "Do we really know how we are doing? Our parish has so many differences of opinion, do we know if our techniques are working to bridge the gaps caused by the merger? Do we know what we want the consultants to do?"

## A BINDING CONTRACT

Finally, a few days later, the vestry expressed their respect for and confidence in the consultant team and voted to accept a two-month contract. The consultants' job description was still vague at this point, though the terms of the contract were clear. The vestry minutes clearly record the fee agreed upon, the amount of time involved (three days per month), the travel allowance, and the establishment of a liaison committee to work with the consultants. The minutes record a nine-to-three vote in favor of entering a consultative relationship. No one—rector, vestry, or consultants—was very clear about what kind of consultative relationship they had agreed upon, or exactly who would receive what from it. A formal contract and job description were never actually recorded, although there was a letter of agreement, written to satisfy one vestry member's concern about the neighborhood, that listed the terms. The letter specifically instructed the consultants to become knowledgeable about the unique history and development of the Hyde Park-Kenwood community. It spelled out certain learning steps they were to perform, such as talking to community leaders, reading a book on the community, and visiting the local co-op.

Warner White, in reporting the decision to the consultants, said the vestry felt that the consultants' first job for the two-month period was to work with them to "explore and define what their problem was." At the end of October the vestry would review the situation and draw up a new contract if they so desired.

The consultants felt uncomfortable with this agreement because it was not their idea of a parish consultation. They realized that the vestry's expectations and their own were not the same. The vestry seemed to be looking for an outsider to *tell* them their problems and make a report on their history. Megginson and Rathbun saw their own style of operation as enabling the parish to discover its own problems and work on its own goals. They were not willing to give readymade answers and reports. They accepted the contract, however, because they feared if they went back to renegotiate they would lose their client altogether. Even though the agreement meant something different to each party, the consultants felt that it was more important to get a limited contract than no contract at all.

The process of negotiating a contract between St. Paul and The Redeemer and the consultant team was fraught with difficulties. There was a total lack of clarity, which was later to hinder the consultants' work. From the consultants' point of view, the pressure to get a contract meant they were not free to say "no" to a potential client. The parish had different points of view; the rector was supportive of consultation and pushed hard to get a contract, but the vestry did not wholeheartedly accept the idea or feel the need for consultation. The contract itself was vague, and no one party understood clearly who the client was or what specifically was the nature of the consultants' work and the service they offered. Because of these inadequacies, the church and the consultant team began their work on an unsteady footing and ended up with differing and mixed expectations and goals.

The two-month contract began on September 27, 1970, and the first major task of the consultants was to gather information on the parish and the neighborhood for a diagnosis of the parish's problems and needs. Besides interviewing parishioners, Rathbun and Megginson were invited to attend several parish meetings as outside observers, "taking notes of interest for the national church," as the rector put it. The consultants understood this description of their role as prohibiting them from making any comment on how the discussion groups functioned or the way in which members related and worked together. Warner White, commenting on the consultant's role, perceived it as follows:

I did not conceive of a consultant's role in a long-term situation as providing process intervention at a particular meeting for its own sake, but I saw the consultants performing a different function—helping to change our relationship, responsibilities, and expectations. I perceived Marshall and Ann to be in the data-gathering stage preceding action. I do not recall these activities being prohibited by name.

Another involved member commented: "I do not remember that the vestry ever forbade the consultants to speak—that they were not allowed to participate. People were doing a lot of assuming."

THE ROLE OF THE RECTOR

Though the consultants felt they could make no comments, they carefully watched the manner in which War-

ner White led a meeting. Afterward, the consultants and
the rector met informally to discuss the meeting and his
style of leadership. Up until this point in Warner White's
ministry, he had seen his role primarily as an administrator. He explains:

The first six or seven years of my ministry I got pretty badly
beaten over poor organizational work. Since those difficulties
I had been consciously working on administration and organization. As for the personal growth stuff, I didn't worry about
that. Only recently have I felt a need to improve my ability
to work and relate to people individually.

White often seemed to cut people off who disagreed
with him and had difficulty hearing what they said. At
times he seemed unaware of the valuable and affirmative
contributions people had made. The consultants, however, found him extremely receptive to change and criticism, and he had a tremendous capacity to absorb their
observations. Welcoming their honest reactions, he was
able to look at his pattern of dealing with people and consider more productive alternatives. He consciously worked
on his style of leadership. More important, though, White
made a drastic change in his style of ministry.

I now spend much more time in parish calling, hospital visits,
and counseling, and much less time in administration. Most of
all, I really know that I am loved here. All my life that's been
hard for me to believe. Marshall and Ann have helped me see
that.

The importance of the consultants' work with the rector
cannot be overstated. It proved, in fact, to be one of the
most important contributions they made. The consultants
were able to support Warner White and also to show him
the consequences of his authoritarian behavior. Because

of their personal support, White was freed to let go of administrative duties and spend more time with his people.

## TEMPORARY SETBACKS

Besides working with the rector, the consultants also met regularly with a liaison committee of the vestry. This group included the rector, the parish secretary, and several vestry members. The function of the liaison committee was to support the consultants and to provide a link between them and the vestry. At one of their first meetings the group discussed parish problems and hopes for the future. Several members began to share their personal needs. Some wanted to see their church really come alive. Others observed that there was a lack of joy in the committees. The rector and one black woman began to talk honestly and seriously about the racial problems at St. Paul and The Redeemer.

The consultants felt encouraged at this point because they saw the group come to life. But immediately after this fruitful discussion the liaison committee members became very formal and told the consultants to go out and do their job; that is, go out and find a problem. The group saw no connection between what they had just been discussing and the consultants' contract. Megginson commented later that that particular meeting "blew his mind."

At this time the consultants began to feel the serious bind they were in because of their agreement. They had interviewed members of the congregation, attended parish meetings, worked with the liaison committee and the rector, but they felt tied down as far as helping the parish make any changes. They felt paralyzed because they felt they were unable to speak up at meetings or have any effect on the parishioners. They were seen only as outside research observers gathering data for the parish and the wider church. They had not been included in the planning of an important educational meeting. Reviewing their situation, the consultants began to wonder about Warner White's commitment to their work. His initial enthusiasm seemed to have waned. Was he keeping the consultants out? Did he trust them? Perhaps he had different thoughts about the consultation. They decided to meet with him in order to share their anxieties and to express their many questions and concerns.

Warner White was resistant to having a private formal meeting with them. He felt that meeting separately with the consultants would violate their contract with the vestry, and he responded to the consultants:

I do not like to make private agreements on parish matters. Parish matters are parish business to be settled in whatever the appropriate parish body is. PTP consultation is to be discussed in vestry and liaison committee, the latter having been established for that purpose. One of the hazards of trying to de-clericalize in a clerically oriented church is failure to recognize when someone is trying to cut you out of the herd and get you to make the decision without consultation. So, when I get the notion that that is happening, I dig in my heels and say "NO."

After several attempts Megginson and Rathbun finally got together with White in his home. He was reluctant to discuss these questions and firmly upheld the vestry's directive to go out and gather data on a problem. Consistent with his administrative stance, he earnestly wanted to follow the vestry's instructions. Finally he consented to writing down his goal for the parish: To change the style of leadership to more black participation. One of the consultants describes the conversation as follows:

Warner was very cautious and kept reminding us that the vestry had commissioned us to go find a problem. He did not want us to work on the goal he stated, but we were to go find another goal. Toward the end of that difficult meeting, Warner gave us a list of people we might interview. He became very excited and animated over the prospect of interviews, he wanted to find out what parishioners were thinking and he wanted to get a history of the parish.

After receiving the rector's advice on people to interview, the consultants began an extensive process of gathering information on the parish. Many hours were spent interviewing parish leaders and other members of the parish and staff. A short questionnaire was developed to help the consultants find the parish's goals and problems. The interviewee used it as a point of departure to express his or her feelings about the church and its leadership, and the consultants found it so helpful that they used it with other vestry members and parish leaders. Not only was information obtained but enthusiasm was generated among the parishioners. They seemed to enjoy the opportunity to talk in detail with an outsider, and to learn from the experience. The senior warden described how the questionnaire affected him:

I had spent a year and a half in the parish grappling with what I, and everyone else, saw as problems—lack of goals and purposes, failures of communication. I had begun to sense it was all too "ultimate" for our little vessel, that much of our emotional concern stemmed from simpler problems of leadership —absent wardens, a rector who professed to be democratic but didn't really operate in a way that permitted other voices to be effective. For the first time, with the "leadership questionnaire," I was able to see and speak of this clearly, simply because the questionnaire was phrased in terms that drew this out.

## CONTRACT RENEGOTIATIONS

By the time the consultants had finished these extensive interviews, the date had arrived for them to renegotiate their contract with the vestry. In preparation for that vestry meeting, Megginson and Rathbun met with the liaison committee to go over all the information in order to formulate future goals for the consultation. They categorized all of the data so that the committee could understand more clearly the issues that had surfaced. They used a wall chart and also mimeographed each question and the different responses. The liaison committee carefully developed a goal that seemed clearly to follow from the interview material. They stated it as follows:

. . . to come to the place where we can agree on expectations, not just intellectually but on a feeling level, for the clergy, staff, and laity.

At the December 13, 1970, vestry meeting, the liaison committee presented the consultants' findings and the committee's goals. The vestry minutes record that the members selected one area—leadership—that seemed to be central to the parish's life. They listed their goal in terms of questions:

1) What should be the leadership style of the parish, of the rector, of the vestry and staff?
2) How does the parish make decisions and get business done?
3) Who should do what, when?
4) What are the expectations as to leadership among the rector, vestry, congregation, and staff?
5) How can we improve in this area?

The liaison committee recommended to the vestry a three-step program in order to work on the above issues. The steps were:

1) A workshop to be held in January with outgoing vestry members and the rector. The purpose would be to build on the outgoing members' experience so far —to find out what had helped and what had hindered their work.

2) A second workshop to be held at the end of January with the new vestry. The purpose would be to orient the new members to the work of the previous vestry and to work on the area of leadership expectations.

3) The third step would involve transmitting the work of the above two workshops to the congregation at large and concurrently to interview as many parishioners as possible who were not in leadership roles.

One of the committee members explained the rationale for using consultants—to set up and lead the two workshops and help determine how to accomplish the third step. After a thorough discussion, the vestry voted nine to three in favor of a contract. The work was to be accomplished within the two-month period of January and February, 1971.

This second contract, though also not formally recorded, was very specific about expectations and job description. It was clear that the consultants were hired for a specific purpose, to carry out a specific task. There was general agreement between both parties, the church and the consultants, on their job for the next two-month period.

## VESTRY WORKSHOPS

The consultants, eager to begin work on the parish expectations and vestry-rector roles, began planning with the liaison committee for the first workshop. On December 31, Megginson and Rathbun presented a questionnaire to the liaison committee in order to get more specific information from the vestry for planning the workshop. The committee gave enthusiastic approval and volunteered to take the questionnaire to the vestry that very day, New Year's Eve, 1970.

The consultants spent many hours studying the information from vestry members. The team, in designing the work, noted how many comments were repeated by different people. Again they arranged the material in large areas for the vestry and rector to look at. One of the most obvious problems that appeared was the problem of implementing decisions. Since job descriptions for the rector and vestry were unclear, it was difficult to determine who was responsible for seeing that actions got carried through.

On January 9 and 10, 1971, the vestry, rector, and consultants came together for the first workshop. The vestry had specifically instructed the consultants to deal during the workshops only with work; *i.e.*, specific problems or tasks. As the consultants put it: "The vestry wanted no part of anything that had to do with sensitivity training or anything on a feeling level."

The groups began by looking at all of the organized material and then exploring their roles as vestry members and how they functioned as individuals. They also divided into small groups to list criteria for a good vestry member. The two chief characteristics identified were:

1) The ability to perceive and represent the parish constituencies.

2) The ability to see tasks through, both as a group and as individuals.

These two abilities were discussed in detail and specific plans were made to help both vestry and rector reinforce and complement these essential tasks. The group then tested out their ideas while dealing with a concrete problem—the parish building and maintenance job. Together the rector and vestry were able to come to a clearer understanding of each task. An important part of the workshop for the rector was examining a serious misunderstanding about expenses for the new vestments required by the liturgical changes of the previous month. As Warner White put it: "We learned how to make a complete decision—policy, cost, who does what, timetable, etc."

The workshop ended with a sense of accomplishment and future direction. One member commented, "It was a relief for me that we finally examined our function—our system of decision-making and delivery. All of it was important!" Another spoke about how "enabling" the consultants had been, not only in structuring the meeting and providing the mechanics to discuss issues, but also by helping them to see their malfunctions and to work toward achieving their goals. Looking back at the event several months later, Warner White, as rector, felt that the workshop had set in motion a marked shift in the leadership of the parish. He put it this way:

I suddenly became aware that I needed to be very careful not to trespass—that all of a sudden there were all these vestry people out there working like mad and insisting on their prerogatives. From a position in which I constantly felt the need to be prodding people on, starting things myself, holding everything up to keep it from falling in, now suddenly I have to get out of the way, run to catch up and get on board, stand and cheer on the sidelines. My new anxiety is how to help it take, how to become free myself to do what I can do and not just become a functionary. If I am not the fount of all wisdom and all decision, neither am I merely one who carries out vestry decisions. I want to do what is uniquely mine to do.

Now that the vestry and the rector were communicating and understanding each other's expectations more clearly, the consultants turned their attention to their second goal: orienting the new vestry members to the learnings of the previous vestry; and building on the former vestry members' hard work and accomplishments. In essence, the goal was to build a basis for smoother operation of the parish. Again, the consultants administered a questionnaire to the new vestry, asking for their expectations as vestry members. As one member put it: "The questionnaire started us working on our most knotty problems."

On January 30, 1971, the rector and the new vestry spent the day together again to look at their jobs. They focused particular attention on how they could affect the entire parish. Their first task was to begin to get to know each other. The consultants asked them to pair off and share something in their church life that had been moving or meaningful. The groups then identified and discussed their personal stake in the work of the vestry and what they wanted to see accomplished. After finding out about each other and their goals, the group listed the kinds of support they needed from each other.

In the afternoon the new vestry took a task from the former vestry workshop (January 9), that of "perceiving and representing constituencies." They worked at finding ways to implement this goal concretely in the parish. At this point Megginson and Rathbun commented on a strange phenomenon that they had noted throughout the consulting period, that no one seemed to know the parish goals despite all the time and energy spent on this matter.

Together the group began to talk about implicit goals that were often assumed but not spelled out. One of these was that St. Paul and The Redeemer had chosen, over the course of the past year, to be a pastoral, family-oriented parish rather than a social-action parish. It had also concentrated on revitalization of worship. By clarifying these underlying goals it was hoped that the parish could secure a stronger sense of identity.

St. Paul and The Redeemer had, over the years, developed goals by choosing certain programs and by emphasizing certain interests more than others. Though Warner White was committed to a vigorous social-action stance, being very involved in community affairs and in civil rights work, he did not have the all-embracing concern for socal action that Joe Dickson, the former associate rector, had. Since Dickson had left St. Paul and The Redeemer, there was no professional leadership whose primary commitment was to a neighborhood ministry. Over a period of time, the vestry, as the decision-maker for the church, voted down social-action projects and emphasized instead creative and rich worship experiences. Warner White, growing in his pastoral ministry, noted that the parish's style was similar to that of the nation in general. In the last five years, there has been a waning of interest in social activism, a revival of liturgy, an increased interest in things religious, and a certain inward focus. All of these factors had influenced St. Paul and The Redeemer, and with the aid of the consultants, the vestry was able to identify the goals and clarify the life style of the parish.

In the evaluation session of the workshop, many vestrymen expressed how useful and productive their day together had been. "We were set to work on jobs of concern to us. I felt we tackled them seriously and came to conclusions which we can now follow through." "The workshop had had immediate and auspicious results—one of

the more important being the willingness to work hard."
"People seemed to feel they were accomplishing something
now and not just spinning their wheels."

The senior warden saw the workshop as giving the
vestry, and to some extent the whole parish, a productive
self-consciousness which may have altered and increased
the participation of individual parishioners. This self-consciousness led to some of the work of the wardens and
vestry in examination of roles, organization, and effectiveness. All of this supported the rector in his view of the
parish as a group in which it is possible and desirable to
operate by consensus. Cajsa Elo describes the impact of
the workshop as follows:

I see the workshops as turning points for the vestry. By
this time the vestry had spent a solid year working on 1) the
planning committee's set of cosmic goals, and 2) on Warner
White's job description. What happened at these workshops
was that with the help of the consultants' excellent design and
on-the-spot leadership, the vestry finally got a chance to work
*on itself,* as well as rector-to-vestry, vestry-to-rector, and staff
relationships, which were also considered. In the process of
these two workshops the vestry became aware not only of its
implicit goals but of *who it was.* This awareness, and the
change the rector was undergoing, has altered the whole
course of events, and is, I believe, the most significant result
of the consultancy here.

There seemed to be a change of mood in the parish as
a whole after the workshops. Again, the rector put it this
way:

The mood is one of excitement, amazement, jubilation, wonder-
ment—where is the vestry going? I am no longer having to
drag it along, beat the horses, constantly stay awake to see
that it is on the road. Now the problem is to find my new role,
to see that my drivership is not simply replaced by another

drivership. We need to be more like a migrating tribe, each person with his road responsibilities and his joys of travel.

MEMBERS' EVALUATION

After the second vestry workshop, an evaluation of the consultation was conducted with the liaison committee and the senior warden. During the past year the liaison committee had worked closely with the consultants, not only planning and interviewing parishioners and leaders, but also examining the particular needs of the parish. The evaluation was extremely positive, with the liaison committee members feeling that the consultation had been most productive and helpful in getting the parishioners to work better together, increasing the morale, and developing an organization more dependent on lay participation and leadership.

On March 29, 1971, after the two workshops, the liaison committee, the rector, and the consultants met for the purpose of giving feedback—principally to the rector. Since the summer of 1969, Warner White had been participating in various human relations labs. The consultants' personal feedback to Warner White, the work of the liaison committee, and the vestry workshops had all reinforced White's move from an emphasis on administration to more people-oriented, pastoral work. Typifying this was the fact that White was spending far less time on paper work and more on house calling and counseling. He had made a conscious effort to change his directions. The final meeting of the liaison committee and the rector with the consultants proved, in the rector's opinion, to be the single most important event of the entire consultation. White shared with the group his own specific feelings and needs regarding the wardens and the vestry and the parish secretary. He spoke of the kind of emotional support he wanted and the way it could be provided. In turn, the liaison committee members spoke of their personal needs in relation to the rector, the kind of emotional support they wanted, and how it could be expressed. Various ideas were brought up:

1) The vestry avoids important issues that have a lot of emotional weight around them, and spends a lot of time on trivial points.

2) The vestry suppresses its anger rather than argue points out.

3) The group recommends that the rector help make it possible to discuss touchy issues openly and without too much emotion.

4) The vestry spends fruitless hours hammering away on some point very important to one person.

5) The vestry does not feel free to express itself about certain important issues, and avoids issues which it considers too touchy. Members fear they will be out-voted.

6) It could save the rector time if the vestry would risk presenting programs and possibilities instead of waiting for the rector to fish for them.

The consultants saw the meeting as generating a great deal of feeling and opening all sorts of doors for the future. Warner White saw it as instrumental in his decision to get more training in pastoral care. This was the final meeting with the consultants.

In the summer of 1971 the vestry met to go over the PTP consultation to discuss whether it should be continued or not. They received the useful report from the liaison committee and discussed among themselves their feelings about the consultation. There was a great difference between the vestry's evaluation and the liaison committee's evaluation. The liaison committee clearly understood the work of the consultants and was involved and committed. On the other hand the vestry could never have been considered "on board." One member of the liaison committee explains how she views the difference:

The liaison committee was, I think, an almost too elite group, considering that two of its members were staff personnel. It did not fully represent the vestry. PTP and the committee came across as projects of the "boss" rather than of the vestry. This meant that from the beginning of the consultancy, the rank and file vestry members were not really involved and hence did not have solid commitment to the PTP concept or to the contract; they did not even thoroughly understand what it was all about. There was also not enough contact between consultants and people or between liaison committee and vestry. The consultants' routine leg work (follow-up, paper work, scheduling, communications) seemed somewhat haphazard and last-minute. Probably only the rector was informed as to what stage they were in, and sometimes not even he knew. Certainly the vestry didn't know.

The feelings of the vestry members varied a great deal. Several seemed to be quite hostile about the consultation, saying that they did not really understand what it was all about and that they wanted a research report from the consultants. Another put it this way: "I have recognized that PTP has been extremely valuable to us, and to me personally, but I feel that at this point we've got to 'do it ourselves.' In some ways I feel over-consulted." Still another representative feeling was that they could have done it themselves. "The trouble with the PTP consultancy is that the vestry had been like a patient with a therapist, not like a client with a consultant. Just as a doctor does not tell you what he is doing, so PTP has not told us. I felt the consultants always had a hidden agenda."

Other people felt they had benefited greatly and that the consultation resulted in more effective vestry work. Still others felt that the consultancy was only a matter of personal friendship with the consultants. The rector continued to stress his own personal gratitude for the consultation. He felt that there was a definite difference in his relationships in the parish. He felt that the parish's morale was much higher and that the vestry and church organizations were working better together.

One of the participants most involved in the consultation reflected on its effects:

Regardless of the misunderstandings, confusions, poor communication at times, and lack of commitment by the whole vestry, etc., I think that the PTP consultation has taught us a lot. The effects of these workshops are continuing. One example is the way in which the vestry approached and worked on the proposal drawn up by the Christian Education Study Commission to establish a Parish Board of Christian Education—which was, in fact, implemented early this year. The vestry was not about to rubber stamp this proposal and insisted on studying it, being especially concerned about the relationship of the board to the vestry—who was going to do what. And it is still concerned. Another example is the setting up of the Music Program Committee, which has put on very successful concerts this year. It gets "watchdogged" like you never saw. In this connection, it is most interesting that the vestry has made great use of the Berne theory of contracts, which the consultants introduced at one workshop, even though many members have had only negative things to say about it and don't "see the use of that thing, whatever it is." The vestry has now a sense of its own identity, authority, and responsibility, which it did not have before. It is still working on all of that, and will continue to work on it. I credit the PTP consultancy with helping the vestry in the process of becoming aware. Indeed, I think the process itself is as significant as the results, if not more so. And all the human factors—good, bad, and indifferent—are important.

From the more distant perspective of Project Test Pattern in Washington, D.C., during the Chicago consultation, PTP received only very brief and erratic reports from Megginson and Rathbun. Staff members in Washington did not move in to offer support or push to find out what was going on. As the consultation ended, PTP prodded them for material, but with little success. Since PTP did not develop adequate communication methods that would keep in touch with the consultants, it was unaware of the pressures the consultants were feeling and did not make consultative or other assistance available to the team when it might have been useful. PTP's understanding of the importance of support systems for consultants was reinforced by this experience.

ISSUES AND LEARNINGS

1 THE POWER OF HISTORY

St. Paul and The Redeemer is a product of its eventful history. The parish has been influenced and molded by its past—the events, the people, and the forces of an earlier period. Its history holds difficult and often painful memories. Some of these support unresolved issues which continue to cause tension and stress. The story is complex in that it incorporates two separate histories—the life of St. Paul's Church, and the life of the Church of The Redeemer. These two proud parishes merged, and then spent years working for unity—one history. One of the rectors left the parish, certain parishioners also left and at the same time new people joined the church. The present rector also began to change his style of leadership. Consultants were hired providing outside help and support for organizational change. Just as the nation as a whole shifted styles, so did the congregation. Its neighborhood changed, being influenced by the University of Chicago and neighborhood groups. All of these factors make up the history of St. Paul and The Redeemer and make the church what it is today. Though St. Paul and The Redeemer never forgot its history, many aspects of its identity and style were assumed, subtle, and taken for granted. With consultation, the vestry was able self-consciously and specifically to look at its life style and spell out its goals as a church. By knowing its history and being aware of its style, the rector and the vestry were able to identify their respective roles and what they expected of each other.

## 2  THE DIFFICULT TASK OF MERGER

The story of St. Paul and The Redeemer shows that two separate congregations, deciding to give up their individual identity and form one parish, need to be prepared for a difficult life together. Merger is a serious, shaking event! It takes years of hard work and sheer stamina to unify two separate congregations. The problems are deep-seated, complicated, and highly emotional. Some issues remain unresolved. The creation of a new identity for St. Paul and The Redeemer was a slow, often painful and exhausting effort. Because they have experienced the trauma of a merger, and have had an opportunity to become more conscious of the meaning of this trauma, the people of St. Paul and The Redeemer are even more aware than ever of their history and identity and its influence.

## 3  THE INFLUENCE OF THE ENVIRONMENT

St. Paul and The Redeemer's physical location influences and affects its life. It cannot exist as an island. It is not immune to its surroundings—the South Side of Chicago. At times it has opened its facilities to the neighborhood and at times it has locked the doors. Either way, it cannot be unaffected by its neighborhood. As a part of the neighborhood, St. Paul and The Redeemer pays attention to its environment and is moved and changed by what goes on around it. Church doors are locked; curtains are drawn; thefts occur. Individual parishioners are active in community affairs, yet the Church as a corporate body is not socially active. Just as the church's neighborhood, Hyde Park-Kenwood, is a middle-class, interracial, moated community, St. Paul and The Redeemer is a middle-class, interracial, ingrown congregation. The neighborhood and the church share styles.

### 4 CLEAR AND ADEQUATE CONTRACT IS CRUCIAL
*Consultants Need to Be Able to Say "No."*

Megginson and Rathbun were trained briefly by Project Test Pattern and asked to develop a contract. The pressure they felt to get the job influenced them to settle for an inadequate contract. At times it looked as if PTP was the client, which put them in a "selling" stance with the parish. At one point, realizing that the parish saw their job as research and training, not consultation, the consultants considered renegotiating but felt that they would lose the contract. Eager to help PTP, they did not feel the freedom to say no and accepted the severe limitations.

### Consequences of a Limited Contract

Lack of Involvement—During their initial two-month contract the consultants were instructed to gather data and diagnose the problem. They felt severely limited by their job description as researchers. They felt that the data never became the parish's own material and that they were never able to establish a collaborative style of operation because of the contract. The parishioners saw themselves as external to the data and did not see the accomplishments of the consultation.

Lack of Trust—The consultants accepted the vestry's decision that they not be allowed to make comments at meetings. The only time they could actually work with the parish leaders was at workshops. The consultants felt they needed additional time and were unable to get this. Even at the workshops they felt tied down because the vestry gave them instructions about what they could and could not do. "Deal with work only" was the rule—and yet the consultants were aware of the need to deal with what they considered the real issues, which were interpersonal relationships. They accepted the unreal limits. The consultants did not renegotiate the contract. They never confronted the vestry. Since no one leveled, there was miscommunication and misinterpretation, along with a lot of second-guessing of positions, which caused distrust and suspicion.

## 5 KEY FACTORS FOR CHANGE IN THE RECTOR

Without the willingness of the rector to look at his style of leadership, to change and grow, no change in vestry leadership, lay participation, or administrative style would have taken place. Warner White had a tremendous capacity to take feedback and develop alternative behavior. At the same time the consultants were able to give him support and direction in his change. The most positive effects of the consultation came from the openness of the rector and the consultants' support of this openness.

## CONCLUSION

The case of St. Paul and The Redeemer provides many significant learnings about parish dynamics and consultation. One overall way of looking at these learnings is from the perspective of power and influence. This case demonstrates the different types of power that influence parish life: the power of history, the power of environment, the power of outside consultants, the power of a contract to help or hinder efforts at change. The story of St. Paul and The Redeemer not only points out the "given" powers that form a parish's identity, but it also shows both the difficulties and the opportunities that come with choosing to change a parish's life and employing new "powers" to accomplish planned change.

# 2

# THE STORY OF THE CHURCH OF THE PEE DEE

## TOWNS AND CHURCHES IN THE PEE DEE

Four very small, fiercely independent towns, closely connected to each other by flat tobacco land, make up an area of South Carolina known as the Pee Dee. This northeastern region is approximately 50 miles from the beaches and gets its name from two rivers that run through it: the Little Pee Dee and the Great Pee Dee. In the past, the Pee Dee has been mostly an agricultural region with large amounts of tobacco, soybeans, and cotton. In the last 15 years, major industries have moved into the area, providing greater economic stability. With the exception of the public schools and some businesses, there is no racial integration in this half-black, half-white area. When voluntary interracial meetings take place, they are held either in government-owned buildings or in the Episcopal churches.

Among the small towns of the Pee Dee are Marion and Mullins in the south, and Latta and Dillon in the north.

The inhabitants of each are fiercely loyal to their own towns and jealous and mistrustful of neighboring communities. Town rivalry has been especially evident in local high school sports, and has carried over into the local churches. The Episcopal churches of Marion and Mullins or Dillon and Latta have had little to do with each other. Each views the other with suspicion.

### The Church of the Advent

The largest of these four towns is Marion, whose population is approximately 8,000. Marion was once one of the most beautiful towns in South Carolina because of its

courthouse and public square. The town was named after Francis Marion, who lived in the area and fought in the Revolutionary War. The rivers and swamps are now a major recreation area for folks in Marion. The men belong to river clubs and every Wednesday or Thursday night they meet for cards, drinks, and dinner. During the spring and summer many businesses close on Wednesday afternoon because of the hot weather, and many residents go fishing. One long-time citizen describes Marion, previously a sleepy town, as a very lively, active place with lots of friendly people. As he put it, "I don't know of a better place to live."

The local Episcopal church in Marion is the Church of the Advent. Located on Main Street, Advent had 77 active communicants in 1973. For many years the Church of the Advent had full parish status in the diocese, but four years ago rising costs forced it to ask for financial aid from the diocese, and it has thus become a mission. Being a mission means that the church has to accept a clergyman sent by the bishop.

## Christ Church

Seven miles from Marion lies the smaller town of Mullins, with a population of 6,000. Mullins has one of the largest tobacco markets in South Carolina and in the world. During the six-week tobacco season of July and August 1972, over one million pounds of tobacco passed through Mullins each day. The sales amounted to over 50 million dollars.

Christ Episcopal Church, located on the main street of Mullins, was closed in 1934, reopened in 1942, and has been struggling to exist ever since. For many years the church shared a minister with Dillon and Latta, and members of Christ Church served as lay leaders for Sunday services. At one point, every office and duty was held by

one layman who kept the church going while it was being financially supported by the diocese. Today Christ Church has 18 communicants, although there are more Episcopalians in town. One parishioner explained that the Episcopalians who moved to Mullins went to the Baptist or the Presbyterian churches because Christ Church was so small that it had little to offer. There was no Sunday School, no youth group, and no full-time minister. On Sundays only a handful of people came to church.

### St. Luke's Church

In the northern part of the Pee Dee is Latta, a very small town with a population of 2,000. It is a family-oriented community with a slow, relaxed style of life. Latta is 15 miles from Mullins. Its rival town is Dillon, seven miles away. There seems to be a vague memory of an ancient disagreement between Latta and Dillon, yet no one is clear about what caused it.

The Episcopal church in Latta is St. Luke's. Sixteen years ago a group of parishioners broke away from St. Barnabas's Church in Dillon and started St. Luke's. The

parishioners speak with great pride about their church. A small group of people bought the land and worked hard to pay for a church building and to keep it going.

St. Luke's major problem has always been its small size. In 1973 it had 18 communicants. Though the congregation is a close-knit group, it has continually struggled because of lack of members. Some members feel the Episcopal church in Dillon County would have been stronger if the Latta and Dillon churches had remained together. As one member put it, "I don't think St. Luke's ever should have been built."

### St. Barnabas's Church

The fourth town in the Pee Dee, Dillon is also located in the northern section near the North Carolina state line. It is seven miles from Latta and significantly larger, with a population of 6,700. Dillon is a business-centered town with a railroad running through it. An outsider familiar with the Pee Dee area describes Dillon as a more transient city with fewer family roots than the other towns. It is a growing town with many industries. Shopping centers are being built and the town is considering enlarging the private air strip so that the jet planes connected with industry can land there. Though Dillon and Latta are in the same county and share the same courthouse, there is little communication or exchange between them.

For many years St. Barnabas's Church in Dillon shared a minister with the nearby Episcopal church in Bennettsville. After that time St. Barnabas worked hard and built a rectory and parish house. More recently, the church shared a minister with the Latta church. The fact that he lived in Dillon gave St. Barnabas parishioners a stronger sense of identity in the community. Over the last three years a continual complaint by St. Barnabas has been an inexplicable drop in attendance and participation. The total

number of communicants in 1973 at St. Barnabas was 53, yet church attendance has rarely exceeded 15.

## A *Discouraging Situation*

Though the churches are in the same diocese and within twenty miles of each other, their parishioners are spread out over an area of 120 square miles. These four mission churches have several factors in common that influence their lives. The Pee Dee is a strongly fundamentalist part of the state. Church revivals prosper. The Episcopal Church is in competition with fundamentalism and "old time evangelism," which has a strong appeal to local Episcopalians. Three of the four Episcopal churches were started in the late 1890s as "gentry" churches, but they are no longer the "social" churches in town. While the local Baptist, Methodist, and Presbyterian churches continued to gain members, the Episcopal church has not grown. As one person remarked, "The churches have not welcomed newcomers in the past; in fact, it has not occurred to them to grow."

While the Episcopal Church in the Pee Dee is indeed in the minority, the other local churches group Episcopalians with Roman Catholics, who represent the smallest denomination in the area. This Roman Catholic image makes other church people suspicious and mistrustful of the Episcopal Church. They associate the Episcopal Church with the Pope and Catholic beliefs, which they see as contradictory to their own beliefs. When the Roman Catholics in Dillon built a hospital, many Protestants refused to use it.

One parishioner remarked:

We are also seen as conceited and hypocritical. Other churches frown on us because we dance and take a drink. Not until recent years have people in the Pee Dee held cocktail parties in their homes. Before, men would have to go to the river clubs to have a drink.

## A Question of Survival

By 1970 the four Episcopal churches were low in membership and resources. The morale was also low, and the small size of the congregations caused very concrete problems. One problem noted in many places was a lack of fellowship. As one parishioner explained, "It's very hard to feel fellowship when three people are in church on Sunday and the church is vacant the rest of the week." Another explained: "At Easter I'd drive 35 miles to Florence, South Carolina, because I couldn't bear the smallness. On regular Sundays I'd be scared that the service would flop because no one would come."

Another major problem of all four churches had to do with finances. "We realized that in order to pay our bills and have a minister, we needed more people," explained one senior warden. In 1970 the diocese was giving $9,000 to the four parishes and supplying two clergymen—one for Marion and Mullins and another for Dillon and Latta. There were many different feelings about the parishes' relationship to the diocese. Many active members were uncomfortable in their dependent state and wanted to be free of it. One member said: "The bishop is an excellent person, but we felt that we were tolerated by him, that we were a burden to him."

Other members of the four churches were aware of their financial dependency but it did not bother them very much. The diocese had always come through. A few members had read about the overabundance of ministers and couldn't understand why the diocese could not give every parish, no matter how small, a clergyman.

In 1970 the Rev. G. Markis House, a recent seminary graduate, was placed in Marion by the bishop of South

Carolina, the Rt. Rev. Gray Temple. He was to serve both Advent Church in Marion and Christ Church in Mullins, seven miles away. He would hold one service at each location every Sunday. In the northern part of the Pee Dee, the Rev. John Buchanan served Dillon and Latta, also holding separate services for each mission each Sunday.

## The Diocese Initiates Changes

In January 1971, John Buchanan accepted another parish call and left Dillon and Latta. Bishop Temple and Canon George Chassey, chairman of the diocesan Department of Missions, met with the congregations from Dillon and Latta, to discuss their future. Canon Chassey also met with Marion and Mullins in the south. Since the diocese could not continue to pour money into these missions, several alternatives were suggested. The churches could go back to using lay readers full time or they could try a new approach called clustering. This new effort involved sharing one clergyman among the four churches and pooling their resources. The bishop and the canon emphasized that this clustering effort would be on a trial basis. If any mission grew strong enough to become a parish by itself, it was free to leave the cluster at any time. From the diocesan perspective, using only one clergyman was a pure necessity, because of the financial drain of paying two salaries and supporting four very small places. "The bishop never said we had to do it, but it was more or less a forced agreement. We knew we could not continue as we were. It was either do it or fold up," one member recalls. Each church knew that something had to be done.

## Initial Efforts Toward Unity

The clustering effort began in all four churches on Easter Sunday, 1971. Under the leadership of the rector,

Mark House, over two hundred people showed up for the Easter service in Mullins. Christ Church was packed with people and extra chairs had to be set up in the back.

During the spring of 1971, the wardens of the four churches worked diligently to figure out what cluster meant for the Pee Dee. The diocese had informed them that cluster was a very new concept. They could not give guidelines or advice, because they had no precedent. It was a do-it-yourself experiment. The people were on their own. The diocese would provide moral but not financial support.

The four churches began by putting all their funds into a joint checking account, although their savings accounts were not combined. Each church contributed equally to a "slush fund" to meet the rector's salary and allowances, the secretary's salary, and the office expenses. Many people were leery of this move, fearing that if the experiment did not work, they would be unable to get their money back. An effort was made to open up communications by starting a church newspaper, *The Seed*. Mrs. Emily House, the rector's wife, was the editor, and the paper had local church news, announcements, and, to keep all four chapels informed, the vestry's monthly minutes.

Although these efforts were made, the programs of each church continued to function separately with Mark House trying to keep all four running at once. Each mission held its own church service and used lay readers when House was unable to conduct services. In the summer of 1971, an effort was begun to help the churches work together. The wardens from each church formed an advisory vestry to work out guidelines for the cluster. This was an attempt to discover what the cluster system meant for the Pee Dee. From here on, this group of wardens acted as the vestry of the Church of the Pee Dee.

*Additional Outside Support*

Other events taking place in the Diocese of South Carolina in 1971 were to support the Pee Dee's cluster efforts. The diocesan Department of Missions began a serious study of its mission field, developing a clear policy for helping the missions and clarifying the diocese's expectations of the missions. With financial resources becoming increasingly limited, the diocese could not continue supporting the many small missions, and it began to look at ways to help them become financially independent.

In the spring of 1971 the Department of Missions met with the Rev. Loren B. Mead, to hear about his approach to parish problems. Mead, from his perspective at Project Test Pattern, spoke of the renewal and growth of the local congregation through the use of consultants. Bishop Temple and Loren Mead later discussed the type of person who could serve as a consultant and the training he would need. Bishop Temple, in an effort to provide helpful resources, appointed the Rev. Herbert Gravely as diocesan consultant on missions and sent him to Boston University for two weeks to receive training in organization development consultation. By the early fall of 1971, the diocesan Department of Missions and consultant Gravely were prepared to assist missions in becoming stronger churches.

Herb Gravely, a soft-spoken and very able clergyman, had for many years been the rector of a large congregation in Myrtle Beach, South Carolina. He made a positive decision to shift his style of ministry, and became rector of a small mission in Kingstree, South Carolina. He also began serving as a parish consultant in his free time.

Herb Gravely's wife, Mary Jeane, travels with her husband during 80 percent of his consultative work. Since Mr. Gravely does not have a consultant teammate, he finds it helpful to have his wife serve as an observer who can note how he comes across and how the client is reacting. As Gravely describes his role:

I'm not employed as a process consultant hired by a vestry. Rather, I go where there is apathy, hopelessness, and discouragement. I set forth two convictions. First, God's Spirit is in all of us; and secondly, the church is healthier when this Spirit is used to diagnose, plan, and evaluate the life of the people.

## Problems of Working Together

By the fall of 1971, the four missions of the Pee Dee were not working together. Each mission continued with its own programs and seemed to like it that way. They voted down Mark House's idea of a joint Sunday School because of scheduling problems. One outsider familiar with the Pee Dee described the atmosphere: "They like it this way and they really mean it when they say they don't want to change." The individual missions were satisfied because each was getting its own programs and services led by Mark House, while the diocese was still paying the bills.

From the perspective of Mark House and the diocese, however, the situation was not so satisfying. The diocese was still supporting the missions and working its priests too hard. Mark House was personally "uptight" about the situation to the point where he had to be hospitalized for high blood pressure and nerves. He had even discussed with Bishop Temple the possibility of a transfer. On the other hand, House was receiving strong support from his wife and from the senior warden, George Smith. Smith had been elected by the advisory vestry from among its members. Both Emily House and George Smith were able to listen to Mark House and encourage him in his widespread responsibilities.

In October, Herb and Mary Jeane Gravely went to
Marion to meet with Mark and Emily to talk over what
was happening in the Pee Dee and how Gravely could
be helpful to Mark and the four missions. Gravely describes Mark House at this time: "He was as busy as a jug-
gler, trying to keep four programs in the air at once. He
occasionally pushed them to collision, but usually they
bounced apart again."

After the discussion, Mark House invited Gravely to
attend an October vestry meeting to help the group develop the cluster proposal they had begun in the summer.
The advisory vestry had bogged down and wasn't getting
anywhere. They were talking in circles and seemed unable
to work out a proposal. They were also leery about using
a consultant, feeling suspicious of someone coming in from
outside to tell them what to do. As Mark House described
the situation:

We weren't ready to go. It was like putting a quarter horse
in a thoroughbred race; the quarter horse couldn't care less
about racing. None of us knew at that time what we were
supposed to be doing. The diocese said: "Be one instead of
four." Each mission and town was fiercely independent. We
were all mistrustful and apathetic. I would call a meeting and
only half the wardens would attend. No one knew what to do.

## THE CONSULTANT AS COMMUNICATOR

Herb Gravely met with the vestry for the first time on
October 12 in Latta. After he and the group had become
acquainted, Gravely took great pains to explain carefully
the diocese's position. The word "cluster" was unfamiliar
to the group and had caused some misunderstandings. As
one person said, "I don't like the word 'cluster.' When I
speak of cluster, I think in terms of oysters."

Gravely clarified for the vestry the diocese's understanding of a cluster. A cluster did not mean a forced amalgamation of several missions into one, nor was it a simple "field" for a clergyman to cover. Cluster meant a voluntary association of missions, combining programs, fellowship, and resources and moving toward a collective, nondependent parish status for an area. In discussing whether the churches of the Pee Dee were a real cluster, several vestrymen noted that the Church of the Advent in Marion, since it was the largest and most likely the strongest, was acting as though it were doing the others a favor. For the other three missions *survival* was the word. They were doing anything to stay alive, and they clearly felt that if the diocese cut off funds they would die.

## MOVING TOWARD INTERDEPENDENCE

In November 1971, the vestry and Mark House met again with Herb Gravely to create a policy for clustering in the Pee Dee. The vestry clearly understood that the people of the Pee Dee were responsible for the cluster and needed to develop its form for themselves. The attitude had to be one of interdependence. With these ideas in mind, the vestry broke into two groups—one to write a proposal for the Church of the Pee Dee, the other to list the problems and arguments against clustering. When the two groups came back together, they shared their ideas and then developed a presentation to all the missions. December 12 was set for a combined meeting of the four congregations in Marion.

During the period before the December meeting, communications between the vestry and the four churches had broken down. No reports were made, and rumors were circulating that the diocese was going to close down all four churches. People began to lose faith in the cluster idea and even began to feel animosity toward it. As one parishioner remarked, "We knew the four wardens were meeting together. They should have kept us informed even if only to say, 'There's nothing to report.'"

Before the meeting, Mark House had sent a letter to each family in the four parishes, explaining the purpose of the meeting. Approximately 50 people showed up after church on Sunday on December 12. Herb Gravely, aware of the pressure that had built up and the heavily loaded message to come, told the people of his two presuppositions. People who are to accomplish a plan (like a cluster) must (a) have participated in the forming of the plan, and (b) have adopted the plan for themselves. A consultant is a communication agent only.

Gravely then moved on to explain the background of their coming together. He spoke of the small number of Episcopalians in the Pee Dee and the rising cost of keeping a small church going. Bishop Temple had met with St. Luke's and St. Barnabas the preceding year and had assigned responsibility for these other two places to Mark House early in 1971. This was the initial move toward clustering. Since that time the wardens had been meeting to work out details. They were not trying to hide anything from anybody. In fact, they were now sharing the churches' situation with all of the people of the Pee Dee. The diocese was asking them to begin in 1972 with a united budget. Next Sunday each parish would have a special meeting to discuss the plan and vote on it. After discussion, the meeting was adjournd with a generally agreed upon observation by one person that "We've got to do this! The only alternative is to stay apart and die."

On the following Sunday, each church met and discussed the proposal developed by the wardens. All four adopted the following plan:

In order to advance the work of the Episcopal Church in the Pee Dee area, the wardens of the four churches propose that:

1. the Episcopal Church of the Pee Dee (ECPD) be established;
2. the four chapels remain intact physically and operationally;
3. a member of any chapel is also a member of ECPD;
4. the ECPD should consist of a vestry composed of the rector and three members from each chapel elected by the congregation of the ECPD;
5. there be a united budget and pledges;
6. there be no individual mission committees;
7. the intent be to strengthen each mission so that it will become a parish within itself. We suggest that the decision to become a parish separate from the Church of the Pee Dee be that of the individual mission based on diocesan guidelines;
8. as soon as requirements are met, we apply for parish status as the Church of the Pee Dee.

### SUSTAINING ONE UNITED CHURCH

The year 1972 began with new hope and enthusiasm for the Church of the Pee Dee and for Mark House. In several ways it marked the end of an era. Two major steps forward had been taken by the churches. They clearly saw where the diocese stood in relation to small missions and they began to have a realistic understanding of the changes that needed to take place. The development was partly due to Gravely's skill as a communicator and to the rector's and the vestry's ability to develop feasible alternatives. Without a clear picture of their situation and the leadership of the vestry, the people of the Pee Dee would not have seen the need for changes and would not have moved forward.

Mark House reports that in January, February, and March of that year the situation in the Pee Dee was very good. A united budget was developed and finances were in good shape. A new vestry had been elected with equal representation from the four chapels. Each chapel continued to worship separately, with Mark House serving two places on Sunday and the other chapels utilizing lay readers. On the fifth Sunday of a month the four chapels would hold a joint service.

Up until January, Herb Gravely had held a very tenuous line between serving as an outside consultant and being a communicator from the diocese. In a letter to Loren Mead, dated February 18, 1972, he wrote of his role:

I feel that my effort is best described by the words *communication agent*. The people had never before been asked "What do *you* think?" It was exciting for me to see them look at the possibilities and consider working together. I feel that they still have a long way to go, with many potential stumbling blocks. Mark and the vestry have agreed to seek my continued consultation but I think they'll not ask till a crisis has exploded. It would be so much better to be able to work on problems before explosions. My feelings are mixed. On the one hand I'm tempted to get the bishop to "send" me now and regularly. On the other, it might be best for everyone to wait until they ask for help. In any case, I'm realizing the in-between problem of an internal consultant.

In the summer of 1972 church attendance was low. Lay readers were on vacation and generally less available. The vestry decided to have only one Sunday service for Dillon and Latta, and one for Marion and Mullins. However, with the exception of a men's painting party and the church women's work, no other efforts were made to cooperate. As one person put it, "We were all out for ourselves. We were loyal to our individual churches and not to the Episcopal Church." When a vestry meeting was called, members from certain chapels would not attend. Some parishioners would not attend the joint services.

Mr. Henry Parsley, a seminarian in the Diocese of South Carolina, worked in the Church of the Pee Dee during the summer of 1972. He gave his major efforts to getting to know each chapel situation and he visited every family in the cluster. Parsley reported that certain parishes felt neglected, and this encouraged their independence. Other parishes seemed to be against the cluster, as seeming to strike at the heart of their southern individualism. Parsley also noted an unhealthy apathy and a basic lack of interest in the church for anything more than simply being there. He explained that initiative is impossible when communication is confused and individuals feel defensive and disorganized.

At the end of the summer, George Chassey of the diocesan Department of Missions talked to Mark House about the possibility of a series of workshops led by Herb Gravely. Chassey felt the workshops had been helpful in other places. After receiving permission from the vestry, the rector and the senior warden visited Herb Gravely to find out about the workshops and to fill Gravely in on what had been happening in the Pee Dee cluster. From Gravely's outside perspective it sounded as though the churches' efforts toward unity had reached a plateau. As he saw it, the Church of the Pee Dee had overcome several obstacles. The four chapels had combined their pledges and had developed a united budget. They had begun to experiment with worshipping together. The next step, if the chapels were ever to be unified, was learning to work together.

In order to help the group learn to work together, Gravely suggested a series of workshops in the fall with all four churches participating. In August the vestry agreed

on guidelines, which were recorded in the vestry minutes
as follows:

Mr. Gravely would come up in September for four consecutive
meetings in the four different towns. He would like thirty
people to be present at each meeting. This would be seven
people from each chapel. The same people would attend every
meeting. He wants a few that are *for* what has been done, a
few that are *against* it, and some young people to give their
views. This will be an opportunity for everyone to get their
likes and dislikes out in the open.


PARISH WORKSHOPS

On September 28 Herb and Mary Jeane Gravely began
the first workshop. Mary Jeane served, as Herb described
it, as a "consultant to the consultant." When the Gravelys
arrived for the first workshop, they were faced with an
attendance problem. Thirty participants were supposed
to be present but only 13 women and 3 men showed up.
Gravely decided to go ahead, although he questioned
what the lack of attendance meant. Since the people of
one town did not know the people of the other towns, the
group spent a great deal of time getting to know one another. Herb Gravely then explained some of the "ground
rules" for their work, including such items as listening
to each other, remembering their unity, and accepting
their differences. He also stressed the need to talk about
strengths as well as weaknesses because during hard times,
people have a tendency to see everything negatively. The
group began by thinking through two questions: "What
is the Church?" and "What is the Church for?" In this
way, Gravely gave the participants a structure in which
they could deal with questions they had not wrestled with
before.

Before the second session Herb Gravely met with Loren Mead to discuss the problem of the members' reluctance to become involved. They decided that the vestry needed to understand Gravely's position and reconsider their contract with him. The senior warden was informed and he called an emergency meeting of the vestry. They discussed the difficult situation and also the vestry's failure to be leaders. Gravely suggested that they discontinue workshops and work instead on the vestry's leadership role. Gravely and House left the room so the vestry could make a decision. When they returned, the vestry was asking for both continuation of the workshops, promising better participation, and a vestry retreat that would be held after the new vestry was elected in 1973. Though Gravely left the meeting feeling optimistic, he still had some doubts that they'd really follow through. One vestryman, recalling Gravely's meeting with the vestry, said:

Herb really put the bee on us and we had to come. After all, we had asked him to conduct the meetings, and you can't have success without warm bodies to work on. I had a conflict because the meetings were on the same night as my river club meeting, but I gave up the next four Thursdays to participate in the workshops.

The second workshop proved to be more productive than the first. Twenty-two people showed up, including vestry and other parish leaders. The group shifted from looking at the purpose of the Church to discovering the uniqueness of the *Episcopal* Church. This particular question grew out of the minority status of the Church of the Pee Dee. In a letter to Loren Mead, Herb Gravely described the impact of this question:

The question of uniqueness because we're Episcopalian created a great encounter for the Pee Dee. It has caused me to suspect that we have 10,000 small missions because we have never even asked what our denominational "unique" message is. The ideas of "one is as good as another," "don't disturb other groups," "such a challenge is not right," "we must not steal members," etc. seem to be so ingrained that the chances of gain are given up and decline is accepted. The very idea that we might have something special to which we're to witness shook the Pee Dee group and stirred life. I'm not sure where the idea will lead, but it sho' is fun going.

## SETTING AND IMPLEMENTING GOALS

The third and fourth sessions of the workshops concentrated on setting goals for the Church and planning ways to reach those goals. The answers from the two previous sessions on the Church were grouped into four main areas: worship, Christian education, fellowship, and outreach to others. The strengths and weaknesses of these four areas were enumerated and shared. The large group then divided into four small groups to plan a project to be carried out by December 14, when Gravely would again meet with them to see "what worked and what didn't."

The workshops closed with an evaluation of the experience. The participants felt very positive about the work. Some of their reflections were put on newsprint:

We worked together!
What is the Church of the Pee Dee? has been answered.
Hope.
We can do great things if we think as one.

Some of the challenges/obstacles noted were:

Apathy.
Distance.
How can we keep feeling like one congregation (unity)?

When questioned specifically about the use of a consultant, one vestryman noted Gravely's skill as an organizer with modern techniques. "Sometimes you want something and you don't know what you want. Herb helped us clarify what we needed to do to become one church."

PROGRESS REPORTS

Herb Gravely went back to the Church of the Pee Dee on December 14 to hear reports on progress in the four areas. The worship group decided that the music was one area of great weakness. A choir was recruited and organized. Because of the combined services, there were more people and the congregation could now learn new hymns. More lay readers were also being sought. The outreach committee tackled the problem of reaching newcomers. They mailed newly arrived residents a package containing a letter of welcome with an offer of assistance in locating a church home, a copy of *The Seed* and a copy of the local town newspaper. The Christian education group set up an adult study group to meet the need to learn more about the Episcopal Church. The fellowship group planned one loyalty dinner, instead of two or four, to be held on November 14 in Dillon.

Gravely reported that, as a whole, the groups were proud of the projects, most of all when they succeeded. But they were also pleased for having tried, even when they failed. Gravely remarked:

At this point, I feel pretty good. They have tasted some responsible leadership in the process of the workshops. They feel fulfilled at having worked directly on the Church's purpose rather than on some "busy" work.

He continued his observations in a letter to Mark House:

As I see it, we are at the really important crossroads for the Pee Dee. The potential for the future is great. If the flame is nurtured, much more than mere survival is possible. If, however, the few embers are pulled apart or not kept snuggled up, it will fade out. Mark, you and your feelings about this idea of shared leadership are a key to the possible flame. Unilateral action will smother the experience. Inaction will allow it to fade out. Both of these alternatives are within your power—or so I feel.

OTHER AREAS OF GROWTH

The workshops not only had developed leadership and unity, but they had helped accomplish several specific tasks during the fall months of 1972. Before 1973 arrived there were several other major areas of growth occurring in the Church of the Pee Dee. Some of these cannot be directly traced either to the consultant or the workshop. This clearly points out an important factor for change in the Pee Dee—the commitment and participation of parishioners to the cluster efforts. From the very beginning, the four missions understood that they were on their own. They had not expected any help from the diocese or the national church. Herb Gravely's consultation had been one factor in the change. An equally significant factor was the work of the people. In fact, the two most active areas of church work are the new Wednesday school and the women's work.

Always an active group, the women of the church divided into two guilds, one in the daytime for study, and the other in the evening for professional women working on specific projects. The evening group had more difficulty because of the distances the members had to drive on desolate back roads from one town to another. In October, the women held a bazaar in Marion. Every chapel participated. Though it seemed terribly disorganized to some, it turned out a huge success and earned over $800. (This was a special accomplishment since the women had not prepared their famous plum pudding, a profitable item in past years.) More important than the financial success was the realization that they could work together even though they lived in different towns.

Another step toward unity occurred in the educational program for the children. No one chapel had enough children and teachers to support a Sunday School, and it seemed impossible to schedule one joint school because of transportation problems. For the church year starting that fall, Mark House tried a Wednesday school. He applied some of his learnings, from a Christian Education Conference he attended and from his parish experience, to the Pee Dee situation, and he developed one church school for children on every other Wednesday. School started at four in the afternoon with a worship service, followed by a snack, since most children would come directly from school. Class time was approximately 45 minutes, and was followed by arts and crafts and a light supper. At six o'clock car pools returned the children to their towns. For the most part, Wednesday school has been well received and even attracted children from other denominations. Several parents, however, found it a burden to drive to another town for church school on Wednesday. As one parent put it:

I don't like it [merger and joint church school]. It's not meant to be. But I go along because I want my children exposed to Christianity and I don't want them to have to go to the Presbyterian Sunday School if we aren't going to that church. I wish we could grow enough to have our own church.

## PARISH PRIDE DEVELOPS

Another area of specific growth had to do with finances and fellowship. These two concerns were brought together at the loyalty dinner planned by the fellowship group. The dinner was a great social and financial success, and by the end of the evening, over half of the pledges for the Every Member Canvass had been received and totaled over $15,000. The 1973 budget totaled $27,260 and the Church of the Pee Dee received $21,627 in pledges. The difference will be made up from interest on investments. Beginning in 1973, the Church of the Pee Dee had $8000 in a savings account. Total liquid assets for the year ending January 1, 1973, including savings and investments, amounted to $64,300.

In 1972 the Church of the Pee Dee received $1700 from the diocese and returned $500. In 1973 they received no money from the diocese and gave the diocese $1000. This change in financial security is very important to the Church of the Pee Dee. Not only are they financially independent of the diocese but they are now the givers instead of the receivers. Parishioners take great pride in the fact that they are paying their own way and taking care of their own business. As one parishioner put it: "I told the bishop the other day that he was going to have to move the cathedral from Charleston to the Pee Dee. We are the pride of the diocese." By 1973 another parishioner, who had been leery about the cluster at first, noted that he was 100 percent for it. "Financially it's our salvation. It's the only way we can keep a clergyman."

## BECOMING ONE PARISH

1973 brought another major change for the Church of the Pee Dee. At a meeting on January 14, the congregation, besides electing a new vestry, faced the question of legally incorporating to form one mission, eventually to become one parish. Although the church had operated more or less as one entity for almost two years, the status of the four missions had never been changed legally. A committee of the vestry presented to the congregation the advantages and disadvantages of such a move.

The advantages were:

1. A parish selects its own priest, while a mission is assigned a man by the bishop.
2. Parish status gives the church more prestige in diocesan affairs.
3. One budget with enough money for the parish to be self-supporting would give the church greater independence from the diocese.
4. The Sunday School, the women's circle, and the adult study groups would be large enough to accomplish activities and possibly grow.

The disadvantages were:

1. We will lose four votes at the diocesan convention.
2. We will receive no financial help from the diocese.

The vestry unanimously agreed to merge legally into one mission and apply for parish status as soon as possible. Now it was up to the total congregation to decide. Before adjourning, parishioners suggested other names for their church. The two most popular were Nativity and Resurrection.

One of the most painful drawbacks to becoming one parish had to do with the original charters, which would have to be surrendered. Some of the older members felt that each chapel was losing its identity because of this action. As one member put it, "When the charters go, a lot of people will cry." A dedicated older couple explained their hurt feelings:

We have given so much time over the years to build up this church and we hate to see it wasted. We have services here only once a month and it's an effort for us to go to another town. They might as well close down the church. There is a strong sense of impermanence now.

The Church of the Pee Dee's 40-to-2 vote in favor of the merger can best be described in the lead article of the February issue of *The Seed*:

"THEY WERE RIGHT; IT WAS COLD!"
Someone has been quoted as saying that it would be a COLD day when we'd get these four churches together. Well, we had to shovel away three inches of ice from the sidewalks and steps of St. Barnabas's chapel before the joint service there on January 14, but it happened! At the meeting following the service those present voted overwhelmingly to support the vestry's suggestion that we merge the four congregations legally.

CHANGES CAUSE DISTRESS

Changes in the parish structure had been taking place gradually in order to meet the different needs of the cluster members. Worship services had been combined, Church School had been moved to Wednesdays, and a new vestry had been elected. Each chapel had three representatives on the 1973 vestry. Each vestryman was chairman of a parish committee made up of representatives from the four chapels. Vestrymen were also responsible for keeping their chapel informed about latest plans and developments.

One strong source of tension had to do with parish leadership. Vestrymen were not keeping the individual chapels informed. People often complained about a "sense of looseness." Nobody appeared to be in charge and so the individual chapels seemed to be floundering. This sense of insecurity was especially felt in the three chapels that had no clergyman living in their town. Many felt little personal relationship to the priest because he lived 20 miles away. As one couple said: "We don't see Mark and Emily socially. It's just too far to have them drive up for dinner." Others, though realizing how busy Mark was, wished that he would do more visiting with parishioners. Another expressed the fear that the Episcopal Church would lose its impact in the town because it did not have a local clergyman. Since there was no Episcopal priest in town, the other churches didn't have anyone to contact for ecumenical programs and activities. For example, although Mark House is an active member of the Dillon County Ministerial Association, he lives in Marion county and does the administrative parish work in Marion. When another church contacts Mark, it has to call long distance. Though many active parishioners recognized the difficulty, they were unsure what to do about it. As one person explained:

If I do something for my own chapel, then it's considered sabotage to the cluster. A group of the women wanted to do some spring cleaning in our chapel, but we were told that the entire women's group needed to be a part of this. No one has any clear guidelines about responsibilities. It's very loose.

A small number of people hold a very negative opinion of the cluster. They wanted their own church in their own town with their own clergyman, and felt that the cluster had "taken them over." One member explained her feelings of impermanence:

It can be compared to visiting relatives. We may enjoy it, but are always glad to return home. The cluster makes me feel like I have no roots in the ground.

While the Church of the Pee Dee was legally and structurally moving toward unity, the rector, Mark House, was also changing. Since House tries to divide his services equally among the four chapels, he spends a great deal of time in travel from one to another. He does not have the energy to become active in all four towns and also in all four chapels. Realizing that he can't do all the work, he has moved toward more reliance on lay people. Both in terms of communication and action, lay people have begun to assume more responsibility. As one vestryman put it, "Now people talk to us about their church problems or cluster concerns instead of always going to Mark." Other members who have worked closely with Mark House note a change in the way he works with people. A senior warden said:

Mark has learned to roll with the punches a lot better now. He has learned how to get people to work *with* him rather than for him. Most of the work is done by civilians. Their participation has now become an ongoing sort of involvement.

REFLECTIONS ON FELLOWSHIP

Parishioners from all four chapels have noticed over the past year a change in atmosphere because of the union. They describe it in terms of fellowship: "It has meant a lot to us to get to know people from the other towns. We never had any opportunity to do that before." Another description of the effect of fellowship: "Now we hang around church on Sundays after the service. I hate to go home. I wish we would all bring pack lunches and visit."

Almost all the parishioners agree that a greater sense of community has developed in the Episcopal Church of the Pee Dee. They also claim to be more involved and more considerate than they were before. While some believe they are less self-centered and more concerned about the total group, they also make comments which indicate that they feel more loyalty to their own chapel. One put it this way: "If a parishioner from another town dies, I don't feel the same loss as if he were from my own town." Another active member, while expressing great hope for a unified parish, explained one misgiving he had:

Some day we will probably sell all of the four churches and build one church in the middle of all of them. I've grown up in this chapel, been married here, and my children were baptized here. When I die, I don't want to be hauled up the road for a service and then brought back here to be buried.

DREAMS OF THE FUTURE

While the cluster effort of the Church of the Pee Dee is in its early stages and still has the flavor of an experiment, parishioners are dreaming and talking casually about their future together. One possibility that has received a good deal of attention has been the idea of building one church equidistant to all four towns. Many people see this as a very practical solution to a number of problems. The present Church of the Pee Dee owns nine buildings, the four chapels, plus parish houses and rectories. Their total value is well over $250,000. The upkeep and utility bills on nine buildings is financially draining. Some people also feel that being physically united in one building would foster a sense of unity. It would mean that *everyone* would have to travel to get to church. No one chapel would feel left out or shortchanged. The question of one central plant also raises larger issues. The issue, for example, of how much unity and togetherness there should be remains unresolved. Should their energy and efforts be clearly directed to combining the four chapels into one church or should they work together to strengthen the individual chapels so each could grow and become a self-supporting parish? Though most parishioners see the need for growth, they are unclear about where the growth should take place and how it should happen. The Church of the Pee Dee at this point, in March 1973, has not decided whether the cluster is the true end product or whether it is merely the means to an end.

## ISSUES AND LEARNINGS

### 1 THE DIOCESE CAN STIMULATE CHANGE AND ALSO PROVIDE DIRECTION AND SUPPORT

The four missions of the Pee Dee were aware of their financial straits and were frustrated and discouraged by their small numbers. They knew they needed to change, yet they did not see any alternatives. At the initiative and direction of the Diocese of South Carolina, the Pee Dee missions clearly saw their situation and were given options and alternatives to their present way of operating. Initial efforts were made by the bishop and the chairman of the Department of Missions. Support was later provided by the clear policy toward missions developed by the diocese. The missions knew their own position and that of the diocese. They were also given assistance through the diocesan consultant on mission. The consultant did not tell them what to do but rather helped them figure out for themselves what they wanted. At no point in the overall process of change did the diocese force decisions on the missions. The diocese provided the kind of help that enabled them to grow to independence and yet make decisions on a local level.

2 THERE ARE A VARIETY OF FACTORS BOTH INTERNAL AND EXTERNAL THAT HINDER GROWTH

The Episcopal Church in the Pee Dee is small and is not growing substantially. This rural area of the country has a strong evangelical religious orientation. Churches with a fundamentalist approach thrive, and revivals prosper, while the Episcopal Church, with its "Catholic" image, struggles to keep the doors open. This particular religious orientation is the "given," the "posited," the "fixed" for the Pee Dee area. Town rivalry and southern individualism make up another aspect of life in the Pee Dee that inhibits growth. Residents readily acknowledge their history of intramural suspicion and jealousy, and they carry this rivalry over into the church. All of these factors make up the general atmosphere and approach to life in the Pee Dee. These particular regional ties have had a restraining influence on the Episcopal Church.

3 A CONSULTANT CAN PROVIDE SEVERAL NECESSARY FUNCTIONS WHICH ENCOURAGE CHANGE

Herb Gravely's initial role with the missions of the Pee Dee was that of a communicator from the diocese. He began by helping the missions to face their situation and to understand the position of the diocese in regard to the missions. Later when the churches were having difficulty, Gravely was approached for help with their problems. He conducted a series of parish workshops and provided a structure in which people could voice their opinions, develop goals and work out ways to carry them out. He never gave them answers, he never told them what to do, but helped them organize in such a way that they could work productively and achieve results.

## 4 THE TASK OF MERGER IS DIFFICULT, COMPLEX AND LONG-TERM

It was indeed hard work for four small independent missions to move from a competitive to a collaborative position. After two years of continuing work on the part of the parish leadership, the four chapels have become more unified and are now legally applying to become one parish. It has been a difficult experience. Some people have been hurt along the way. The actual long-term process has had many ups and downs and it is by no means completed.

## 5 THE POWER OF INERTIA IS PARTICULARLY EVIDENT IN THE PEE DEE

It is so easy, every time a small gain is made, to fall back into taking life easy and doing nothing. There is a need for successive inputs of energy, help, and leadership in order to prevent the backward slide. Much work still needs to be done in the Pee Dee. Many parishioners feel that their efforts have just begun. While it has been painful, frustrating, and trying at times, most of the active parishioners see the merger as the one realistic alternative to their situation of few people and very limited funds.

## 6 PARISH LEADERSHIP AND PARTICIPATION ARE ESSENTIAL TO CHANGE

From the beginning, the Church of the Pee Dee understood that the cluster was a new idea. They could not count on the experience of others for guidance. The people themselves are making the cluster work. There is a general attitude on the part of the rector, the vestry, and the parishioners that the people must be involved in order to make the changes work. Parishioners feel a personal responsibility to carry out decisions and plans. The people of the Pee Dee have put an inordinate amount of time and energy into these changes. They consider this factor a key ingredient in their success.

CONCLUSION

In many ways, it is difficult to conclude the case of the Church of the Pee Dee because the story itself is so open-ended. The work has only just begun, and it would indeed be wrong to give the reader the impression that all is said and done. The Episcopalians in the Pee Dee would be the last to say that their church life was secure or that they have now arrived at unity. Such a static wrap-up would not convey their present excitement and strain. Perhaps the most appropriate closing message at this point from the Church of the Pee Dee would be, "We are alive and well. We've got a long way to go. We have cause to hope."

# 3

## THE STORY OF DUMBARTON UNITED METHODIST CHURCH

AN OLD CHURCH CHOOSES TO LIVE IN THE PRESENT

In front of Dumbarton United Methodist Church in Washington, D. C., hangs this professionally painted wooden sign:

> Dumbarton Methodist Church
> One of America's Oldest
> Methodist Societies
> Organized in Cooper's shop 1772
> This Church was built 1849
> Used as Civil War Hospital 1862
> President Lincoln attended
> this Church on March 8, 1863
> It is Methodism's
> mother church of Washington

Inside the door hangs the following sign, which is hand-printed on colored paper:

Dumbarton is an old church which has chosen to live in the present. We are a small congregation seeking new structures for being in mission in the 20th century. Join us for worship Sundays at 11:00 A.M.

The difference between these two signs symbolizes the identity crisis that Dumbarton church has been facing for the past several years.

Dumbarton's external facade is that of a typical "establishment" church, once proud and prosperous, now looking aged and tired. The building is large and imposing, with heavy wooden red doors leading into an expansive first-floor fellowship hall used by the Dumbarton nursery school during the week. One is immediately greeted by play toys and finger-painted pictures hanging on the walls. The worship area is on the second floor and seats three hundred people. Though the brick facade is painted a pale shade of tan, giving Dumbarton a fresh appearance, the total effect of the large, square building is weighty. Dumbarton's architecture is more an old Romanesque than an uplifting Gothic.

Meeting within this structure is a congregation working on the meaning of actually being Dumbarton church and searching for an appropriate stance of witness to the Christian faith. The congregation is very much grounded in the Christian tradition. Preaching and worship, along with programs and training, are biblically oriented and freely use the traditional vocabulary of the faith. By no means a renegade group rejecting its heritage, they are rather a church appreciating and enriching traditional Christianity. Worship is central for this congregation; its life revolves around the Sunday worship experience.

The membership rolls of Dumbarton once numbered in the hundreds, drawn from the prestigious neighborhood of Georgetown. Before the Civil War there were over six hundred slaves on the lists. By June of 1968, the church had around fifteen people attending Sunday morning worship. Most of the members were elderly retired people whose involvement was minimal—church attendance only. Today, in 1972, Dumbarton has just under one hundred members—most of them very active.

The oldest Methodist church in Washington, and one of the oldest churches in America, Dumbarton has recently celebrated its two hundredth anniversary. Though its history dates back many years, the membership is relatively young in age. The present congregation is comprised of twenty-seven young married couples, many with small children; forty-two single people, including some college students; and two teenagers. Georgetown residents are a minority, most of the members being commuters from the Virginia and Maryland suburbs and other parts of the District of Columbia. Many members are employed by the Federal Government.

Of the 1972 membership, at least nine persons were members of Dumbarton before its present pastor came in 1968. Many of the current members are people who were disenchanted with a traditional church and were shopping around for a more innovative worship experience and congregational life. One member describes Dumbarton as "a suburban congregation made up of fairly young, white, Anglo-Saxon Protestants who are attracted to a liberal church and drawn by the feelings of intimacy here."

Most of the present parishioners are very active and spend a great deal of time and energy on church work, although not all feel a strong sense of community. One parishioner said she had tried other churches but did not feel any sense of community. At Dumbarton she felt people really cared. She gave such examples as parishioners taking casseroles to a family with a new baby, or showing concern for a member getting a divorce. Other parish-

ioners felt that Dumbarton talks about community but
doesn't do much. One person said that people were open
and reaching out during the sharing part of worship
services, but at coffee hour he could find no one to talk
to about simple problems—only about grave crises. One
of Dumbarton's most active members explained that it
was the strong sense of community that kept him coming:

At Dumbarton there is a feeling of dependence and community. One couple, after a long absence, returned to church
and the congregation's reaction was joyous. Another man said
he could not attend any longer but would keep up his pledge.
My payoff is in the tremendous amount of support I get. That's
what keeps me operating, and it hasn't come easy. We have
been through tough times. I have a big investment in Dumbarton. I have received a lot more than I can give.

As a total community, Dumbarton church incorporates
many different points of view and strong feelings. Though
members share similar life styles, they do not have the
same priorities, outlooks, and needs. Members agree that
community is important at Dumbarton, yet they disagree
on what community means and how it looks.

## NEW PASTOR INTRODUCES CHANGE

A major stimulus for change at Dumbarton has been
provided by the present pastor, the Rev. Harry C. Kiely.
A forty-two-year-old father of three young sons, Harry
Kiely came to Dumbarton in 1968 because of the possibilities he saw. His former pastorate had been in an inner
city parish that was ninety percent black. Working with
racial struggles had occupied much of his former ministry.
When Harry Kiely arrived at Dumbarton, the congregation had dwindled so that only a handful of active mem-

bers remained. Slowly he began to attract a few young families who were looking for a church that would allow for greater flexibility and congregational participation. With Kiely's skillful leadership, creative worship became a major strength of Dumbarton. It evolved into a form that was neither standard nor "way out," but informal and intimate, allowing for spontaneous congregational sharing. Kiely remembers the focus of his first years at Dumbarton as primarily attracting young families:

People came to church because of worship. That was the lively focus of the parish. I made a conscious attempt to have all of the decisions made at the grass-roots level. Though people felt they could have a hand in the shaping of the congregation, this change sent some of the old-timers away. Within two years, however, new people began to come. They were excited.

In addition to having liturgical skills, Harry Kiely is well received as a preacher, and many parishioners claim his sermons are a major attraction at Dumbarton. Through its rich liturgical life, Dumbarton was able to develop new internal strengths and try new styles of operating.

PARISH EVENTS LEAD TO CONSULTATION

Three years ago Dumbarton church began to change and move in new directions. It had several important experiences which stimulated a felt need for parish consultation.

In the spring of 1970, two years after Harry Kiely's arrival, functional education was introduced at Dumbarton. A small group of parishioners went through a strenuous twelve-week course in functional education. This kind of educational experience represents an existential approach to the Christian faith. Instead of a conceptual approach centering around doctrines, it uses the traditional Christian symbols to look at the way an individual deals with his life. The experience had a stimulating effect on the congregation, although while some felt it provided very honest and meaningful interaction, others saw it as slanted and cliquish. It helped some participants to become more open and honest, and yet it alienated others. Many members became angry. Participants remember this course as a stiff confrontation, something they were not used to.

During the same spring, several crises occurred which exemplified the personal and organizational tensions of Dumbarton's life. The financial problem was so grave that the church faced a question of survival. Harry Kiely told members that he had to have financial support to continue. In May the congregation held a crisis meeting to decide whether or not to continue as a church. Members made a formal decision to continue for one more year. A task force of the Administrative Board was established to work on Dumbarton's financial problems.

Out of this task force came a revision of pledging to balance the budget, a sur-pledge, and tight fiscal control. Members assumed responsibility for financial matters. One of the task force's considerations was a proposal to pull all of Dumbarton's capital into a foundation to engage in social action. The proposal was dropped because it was not feasible. Though this proposal was only one of many steps considered by the task force, it caused quite a stir for the pastor and the congregation. The pastor was threatened and went through serious strife with the people involved. Some parishioners were threatened, feeling that certain members were trying to take over the church.

As tension was mounting in the congregation, Harry Kiely called for a congregational meeting in November, 1970, to give members an opportunity to air complaints and strong feelings. He had heard rumors and wanted to clear the air. Mr. Robert Gell, chairman of the Administrative Board, presided over the meeting rather than Kiely. He did this so that people could feel free to sound off. Gell's policy was that you could only speak from personal experience, and that if you had complaints, you also had to assume responsibility. During the meeting a lot of hostility about functional education came to the surface. People were angry because they felt forced to talk on an extremely personal level. They claimed they were never allowed to have ideas—only feelings. There was little hostility expressed about the pastor personally. Harry Kiely noted that besides the hurt and pain, the worst thing was that the conflict turned into a sort of win-lose situation without the possibility of any reconciliation.

These critical experiences point out the ineffective way conflict was handled at Dumbarton. Polarization occurred among members and the conflict quickly turned into a win-lose situation. In the end, though one group had "won," no one felt satisfied.


INVESTIGATING CONSULTATION

The winter of 1970–71 held fewer crises, and Dumbarton continued to live as a church. In the early summer of 1971, Dumbarton again looked at its internal life and health. At Kiely's instigation the Administrative Board began to think ahead to its fall retreat. The previous year's retreat had not solved the problem of dissension. Kiely introduced the idea of using a consultant on the retreat:

I thought an outside consultant could help us in planning and setting goals. We were not clear on how to plan a program that the entire congregation could buy into. I also felt an outsider could give objectivity. I could not be objective because I'm on the inside. I persuaded the board members to

look into consultation. They appointed a committee to in-
vestigate it.

The committee discussed the possible use of an outside
consultant with the Rev. James D. Anderson, a parish consultant on the bishop's staff of the Episcopal Diocese of
Washington. Mr. Anderson recommended several consultants. Dumbarton contacted one of them, the Rev.
Larry K. Ulrich, a young Church of the Brethren pastor
and consultant from nearby Gaithersburg, Maryland. Ulrich had had training in consultation and had also participated in a week of special training in parish development sponsored by Project Test Pattern, an experimental
project in parish renewal of the Episcopal Church.

On July 28, 1971, the Administrative Board met with
Larry Ulrich to discuss the possibilities of a consultation.
Several important issues emerged which helped clarify
the board's ideas about consultation. Some of the new
understandings were:

(1) Parish consultation is different from sensitivity
training.

(2) Consultation is a long-term process, not a one-shot
program. It is appropriate to do a consultation in steps.
The first step is to gather data and then decide on the
church's priorities. Finally the church makes decisions
about achieving its goals. Ulrich would agree to lead the
Fall Planning Retreat with the understanding that it might
lead to a long-term, in-depth consultation.

(3) The success of consultation does not depend on
the size of a congregation, but rather on the motivation
of the members.

(4) Consultation works best when it involves the whole
congregation. The consultative process would require
planning work with a committee of the board and individual sessions with the pastor.

(5) Project Test Pattern would be interested in information about the consultation and would document the process.

The board voted to hire Larry Ulrich as the congregational consultant, with a fee of $300. They decided on
three goals for the consultation. Consultant Ulrich summarized and explained the board's decision:

Dumbarton wanted to establish goals as a congregation and
then set priorities for the work to be done. These goals would
be both long-term and short-term, and setting the goals
would involve as many members of the congregation as possible. I agreed to help the congregation discover its goals and
then design the board's Fall Planning Retreat to develop a
program to implement the goals.

An initial step in the first consultation at Dumbarton
was to establish a steering committee to work with Ulrich.
This group decided that the congregation would get a
report in writing of each phase of the consultation: data
gathering, priority establishment, and actions by the
board. This would insure a flow of communication.

Before working directly with the Dumbarton congregation, Larry Ulrich met with Harry Kiely to review the
minister's role and his professional goals. They decided a
congregational review and study of the pastoral program
would be helpful.

GATHERING DATA AND SETTING GOALS

On the evening of September 21, 1971, forty-nine members of Dumbarton participated in the first evening of a
parish planning conference. After an explanation of the
work of the two evenings and the proposed follow-up
retreat of the board, the total group broke into five small

groups with every participant given an opportunity to answer three questions.

(1) What is effective and satisfying for me in the life of this congregation?

(2) What prevents life from being more satisfying for me?

(3) What would make life more satisfying for me?

When the total group came back together, the members shared their answers and then arranged the responses according to subjects.

The following evening thirty-four parishioners came back, ready to go to work. Larry Ulrich presented an interpretation of the previous evening's responses:

In examining some of the implications of the responses, it is easy to see that the congregation is most satisfied with fellowship and worship interests. But fellowship concerns head the list of those aspects of the congregational life which prevent satisfaction; and these are followed by community relations and mission concerns, then by leadership concerns. The ambivalence of being the most satisfied with fellowship and at the same time feeling that a lack of fellowship prevents people from being satisfied with the life of the congregation reflects a need for members to clarify personal commitments to each other and to the congregation.

The total group again divided into small groups to work on these five areas. Each group identified long- and short-term goals for the congregation and presented its goals to the total group to set priorities for the ensuing year. These priorities included: defining the responsibility of members of the congregation, including the pastor; developing a realistic financial plan; facing the issue of social change; and setting up a regular evaluation of the organizational structures.

NEW WAYS TO HANDLE CONFLICT

During the second night's large-group session, an incident occurred which could have caused another divisive meeting. After the small groups met, they wrote their ideas on newsprint and taped the paper all over the walls. Larry Ulrich started reading aloud from the newsprint notes, proceeding from left to right. The social action group, who had put their newsprint to the far right, were getting anxious because it seemed likely that they were not going to be heard. Their nervousness was noticed by the large group, which then moved quickly to consider social action. That night, it was decided that one of the four long-range goals would be for Dumbarton "to face the issue of the corporate body being an instrument of social change." This incident represented an important change in the way people dealt with a controversial issue. Previously the issue of social action had caused severe polarization at Dumbarton. Now the congregation was better able to discover ways to resolve the differences.

Kiely reflected on the difference between the atmosphere of this conference and the conference one year before:

Last year's conference turned out to be a tug of war between those interested in social action and those interested in personal development. Though the "personal growth" people "won," no one was satisfied. There was a residue of resentment on both sides. Now, after this recent planning conference, everyone is satisfied. We are all relieved that social action was not ignored and that we were not forced to take any steps we did not want to. This turned into a win-win situation.

Parishioners were aware of the ways the consultant's skills had helped them work together more effectively. One member reported:

Before the meeting I was utterly frustrated. I felt we never got anywhere. After two nights, I at least felt organized to get things done. I was optimistic. We were able to face a central problem of social action. This time, with Larry here, there was real tolerance for everybody. There was something about the way Larry handled it. He set it up and emphasized that every person's opinion was important. This was a new attitude and technique. We didn't have to nit-pick. Everything anybody said was put on the newsprint. The consultation gave us a way to have our say.

## IMPLEMENTING PARISH GOALS

According to the contract, Ulrich was to conclude his work by helping the Administrative Board design a program to implement the goals set at the parish planning conference. In order to do this, a board retreat was held one week after the conference. The retreat began Friday evening with twenty people present for a "trust" meal— an exercise used to bring the group together and raise issues of leadership and trust. For the remaining part of Friday night and Saturday morning, the board divided according to interest into four subgroups to deal with Dumbarton's corporate life, finance, social action, and education. The category of worship was not included because the congregation had indicated such a high degree of satisfaction in this area.

By Saturday afternoon the four groups had identified the problems and named alternative strategies for responding to them. At the meeting of the Administrative Board, each work group presented structures for implementing its strategies. As a total body the board made fourteen major decisions for Dumbarton's 1971–72 program. They assigned responsibility to specific individuals or committees and established a time schedule to report back to the congregation. The board retreat ended with an evaluation and reflection on the consultation. Ulrich concluded by sharing his reactions to their work and by making several recommendations. He said:

The board really worked hard and that's the real key to decision-making. I believe in the small church where people have to relate more honestly with each other. The steps taken by Dumbarton are really beautiful, but accountability is essential. The work that still needs to be done on evaluation and job descriptions is very important and very difficult. I strongly recommend that outside consultation be utilized.

The next day the board presented the fourteen decisions to the Dumbarton congregation during the morning worship service. The fourteen items were not controversial but were ways to get at issues rather than take positions. They included:

(1) Create a monthly "Community Life Sunday"—a day at the church for all to worship, conduct meetings, have dinner and fellowship together.

(2) Establish an educational task force to ascertain needs and provide courses in adult Christian education.

(3) Instruct all committees to set up standards of accountability and responsibility, along with regular evaluation.

(4) Balance the budget.

(5) Sensitize the congregation to social issues and, as a corporate body, face the issue of the church being an instrument of social change.

REFLECTIONS ON THE CONSULTATION

Several things happened following the planning conference and board retreat, all of which were in some way results of the planning process. Harry Kiely identified three specific changes at Dumbarton:

First, there was an atmosphere of euphoria in the congregation for several weeks. There was a sense in which each of us could say, and rightly, "This is my program." The decisions had a genuine grass-roots base.

Second, Dumbarton entered a new era of fiscal responsibility. For three years the church had felt lucky to survive economically. At the time of the consultation, the congregation gave a mandate to the finance committee to balance the budget. At the board retreat, the finance committee threw the ball back to the congregation: "Finances are not the committee's problem. They are everybody's problem." A month prior to the planning conferences and board retreat, the finance committee had obtained $13,000 in pledges. After the retreat, the committee recanvassed under its new mandate, and from the same people obtained $20,000 in pledges. This was an increase of sixty-five percent. Everybody was excited over this victory.

A third change that took place was that new people began to join the church as never before. Previously I had had to buttonhole new people (after they had been around a few months) and urge them to join. After the planning retreat, seventeen people called *me* and asked to join!

> (*Christian Advocate,* "Small Church
> Discovers Itself" by Harry C. Kiely
> December 21, 1972.)

To conclude the planning consultation, Larry Ulrich and Harry Kiely met to review the gains. Ulrich shared with Kiely his ideas on the pastor's style of working and his role in the congregation. These included the idea that Kiely's "moderately mod" style fits the commuter congregation and is open to the Georgetown community. He is obviously loved by the congregation, but his "charismatic" style may encourage too much dependence. Kiely noted that he needed help in clarifying his role and indicated that he wanted regular evaluation of his job.

Reviewing the past months, parishioners also noted changes. "The winter months were definitely exciting at Dumbarton," said one parishioner. "There was a burst of creative effort to meet the goals." The board's recommendations had been sent to existing committees and a date for the completion of their work was announced. The community-life project was started immediately. Regular evaluations were established for all committees. A bulletin board was put up, a Bible study group was started, the social concerns committee set up a retreat, and the education committee was developing study courses.

As Harry Kiely put it:

The atmosphere was very good. Reconciliation was occurring. It became clear that people had not only a voice but also a process by which they could become effective. The entire work became credible because people saw a way for their words to be turned into action. They learned that they could count on this process.

Accountability was a major area of growth at Dumbarton. One member expressed this in terms of the worship committee's work, where she noted a dramatic change:

All of a sudden in January people began really to get work done. Before it had been very lax, a last-minute sort of thing. We began by setting up obligations for members.

She explained other signs of accountability such as meeting even when the pastor could not attend, and asking him to give his sermon outlines in advance in order to plan services. Another parishioner remembers a recent worship service where accountability was the natural norm of behavior:

In church last Sunday, one member stated that the board was going to make an important decision about the graveyard property the coming Tuesday night. Another person got up and said, "How can the board do that when we haven't even heard the proposal yet?" In most groups I function in, this type of behavior would have been out of line. At Dumbarton it would have been out of line for a person not to have spoken up. I trace this back to the consultation because it gave us the openness to do this. If you say you are going to do something, then people will challenge you if you don't do it.

SECOND CONTRACT

The year 1971 was a fruitful one for Dumbarton church. The congregation had worked together in a united effort to establish goals for its ongoing life. At the same time, it had learned new and more productive ways to deal with differences. Using a consultant had helped open and broaden communications between groups. An equally significant change occurred when people realized that they could not only communicate, but translate their words into productive action.

Realizing that much had been accomplished, members of the board's steering committee and the pastor met together early in 1972 to think through ways of building on their accomplishments. Several areas still needed work. The pastor was seeking help with defining his role, and members felt the congregation needed more help with plans and goals. This small group decided that Dumbarton needed additional consultation and decided to present a proposal, mainly for evaluation purposes, to the Administrative Board.

Larry Ulrich, from his position as consultant, commented on this transition:

After this initial phase of consultation when much had been accomplished, Dumbarton went through a period of euphoria, feeling that its life was going along so well that it did not need long-term consultation. I felt that Dumbarton was not interested in looking at future needs. Yet, during the first part of 1972 the church seemed to me to realize that it had not changed as much as it thought. I thought the church was having difficulty implementing goals. As consultant, I let them go on their own and tried not to push them. They needed to be free to make future decisions.

On January 9, 1972, the Administrative Board met to consider a proposal for a second contract. Bob Gell, chairman of the Administrative Board, stepped down from his usual position as moderator to make the presentation. The minutes from the board's January 9 meeting record the following concern:

A member expressed concern that we were avoiding some major issue. She felt that the Gospel was the answer in our progress and that maybe we should probe there . . .

Finally a vote was taken and the proposal passed, though there were a few negative votes.

The specific proposal called for consultative assistance in the pastor-parish relationship and in congregational evaluation and planning. Project Test Pattern and the Baltimore Conference of the United Methodist Church were contributing funds. The board approved a six-month period of consultation and appointed a planning and evaluation committee to work with the consultant, with the understanding that Project Test Pattern would research and document the consultation process.

By the Community Life Sunday following the board's decision, the time had come to review and evaluate the work so far. Bob Gell, chairman of the board, presided over a special meeting at which the congregation heard progress reports on corporate life, education, social action, and finance. The year 1971 had ended with $2500 in the bank and 1972 would begin with the first balanced budget in many years. This was a clear recognition that the responsibility for the financial program was being taken more seriously. Clearly the church's stance had shifted from a struggle for survival to a hopeful, secure approach to life.

After receiving the reports, Gell announced the board's decision to continue the consultation. There was some resistance to this. People felt they did not need any more help. There was a feeling expressed that:

Opinions were aired but the decision had already been made. It had all been worked out. It was as though the board was saying, "You really want to do it because we are getting money from PTP." The board is overwhelming.

There were those who were in favor of the consultation:

I wasn't part of the power structure when the decision was made but I wonder if we did enough to bring everybody on board. I felt surprised by the board's decision, but I liked it. I felt it had been decided and we had to accept it. But then we could have spent weeks making a decision.

## DEFINING PASTOR'S ROLE

After the consultant's work had been agreed upon and presented to the congregation, the pastor-parish relations committee, the pastor, and the consultant quickly got started on the difficult and time-consuming job of clarifying the role of the pastor. All three parties involved—the pastor, the committee, and the consultant—spent many hours during the winter and spring of 1972 working in this area.

Initial work began on January 11 when Kiely and Ulrich met to talk over their expectations and to develop common goals. Kiely, looking back to that work, reflects:

I requested the pastor-parish work because I needed help in getting clear what my role was and what the expectations of the congregation and myself were. I wanted to make sure that these two expectations were clear and that my work could be evaluated. I requested the study not because of insecure feelings but because of my secure feelings at this point. The atmosphere was very good. There was a cooperative feeling. I felt I would get constructive help.

The pastor-parish relations committee's concern was to develop a clear understanding of what the pastor's job responsibilities were. Over the next several months the committee met regularly, often with the pastor and the consultant. They decided that they needed initial input from members of the congregation and administered a questionnaire to discover what the parishioners expected of their pastor.

Kiely, from his perspective as pastor, worked independently to clarify his role at Dumbarton church. During the months of February and March Kiely kept a detailed chart of his time so that he could know exactly where his energy went. He also met with the consultant to identify areas of accountability between pastor and congregation. Working together, Ulrich and Kiely developed three specific recommendations for the committee:

(1) A quarterly review of the pastor's performance to provide accountability and to let the congregation know about his work.

(2) A written agreement outlining the pastor's responsibilities and compensation for the next several years.

(3) Secretarial assistance on a part-time, paid basis.

It was the hope that these recommendations would help provide stability for the pastor and the congregation and at the same time give enough flexibility so that the relationship could change and grow.

After a lengthy discussion, the committee presented its findings to the Administrative Board at a meeting on April 19. Mr. Reggie Cude, chairman of the pastor-parish relations committee, explained to the board the difference between the congregation's estimate of the pastor's use of his time and how his time was actually spent. A major finding was that Kiely spent a great deal of his time in administrative work, keeping the organization running, rather than in pastoral care and education. Larry Ulrich followed Mr. Cude's presentation with a consultant's analysis of the congregational questionnaire. Many people found it difficult to understand. One member, who was trained in data analysis, put it this way:

Larry used informal statistical procedures for the questionnaire. He could have strengthened his arguments if he had used more sophisticated statistical analysis. The chart and analysis of Harry's use of time needed to be simplified. A simple correlation would have expressed differences between the congregation's priorities and Harry's in one figure. Larry did not make use of other techniques available to him. He felt his level of analysis was quite adequate.

To complete its task, the pastor-parish relations committee worked diligently into May in order to complete the Pastoral Role Definition for the Administrative Board retreat of May 19. Reggie Cude later said of the work:

Everything we did during that time was related to the consultation. Defining the pastor's role and clarifying our expectations produced specific results. We all realized that administration was not the pastor's top priority. He needed a secretary. The consultation brought things out into the light and forced us to look at them.

In the late spring of 1972, members of the committee noticed the changes Kiely made in the use of his time. He emphasized teaching, preaching, and counseling, and gave less time to secretarial duties and managing the building. Harry Kiely also participated in a three-week training program sponsored by the Mid-Atlantic Training Committee in order to develop skills in organization development.

Several members of Dumbarton could almost see a personality change in Harry Kiely:

For a long time I felt this place would fold without Harry. Now Harry is not in control. The change has to do with young people coming in who have their own goals. We have stronger leaders now who don't see this church as a one-man show. Harry used to be threatened by anyone who took a leadership role. Because he knows he has been so successful, he is more relaxed now.

PLANNING AND EVALUATING PARISH LIFE

While some parishioners at Dumbarton were developing the role and job description of the pastor, others were working on congregational planning and evaluation. The planning and evaluation committee appointed by the Administrative Board had convened in February of that year and had identified three large areas of responsibility. They were to act as a liaison committee between the consultant and the Administrative Board, and also assume the responsibility of following up on the fourteen areas of work assigned to parish committees at the 1971 fall board retreat. The committee also decided to survey the entire congregation to determine the level of satisfaction with the present church program.

By May the committee had received progress reports from every parish committee on its goals and accomplishments. This was a major step in holding committees accountable for their actions. Mr. Bernie Johnson, a member of the planning and evaluation committee, organized a Program Evaluation Report. In his summary, Bernie Johnson reported on Dumbarton's four major priorities:

(1) *Corporate Life.* The role of the pastor was being well defined by the pastor-parish relations committee, yet work still needed to be done on defining the role and task of a responsible member of Dumbarton church.

(2) *Education.* A variety of opportunities for adult education had been provided during the year.

(3) *Social Action.* The goal of the committee was to sensitize members to social problems and to participate in a corporate project, one yet to be decided upon.

(a) Has social action been something the congregation feels it "ought" to do but lacks the sustained desire to carry out?

(b) If the congregation has a sustained desire to work in the area of social action, what have been the impediments to proceeding?

(4) *Finance.* The budget had been balanced! The finance committee was developing a realistic, long-term financial plan.

The Program Evaluation Report was helpful to Dumbarton because it presented a clear picture of the church's goals and accomplishments. During the same spring, members were looking back on their hard work and feeling the tiring effects. One segment of the congregation expressed feelings of frustration and impatience. They were angry, feeling that people talked a lot but were short on action. They claimed that all Dumbarton had done in the last three years was study itself and set goals, never accomplishing anything. One person exclaimed: "If ever I hear the word *goal* again, I'll scream! Before it used to be *dialogue,* now it's *goal* and *accountability.* We're a very faddish church!" The impatience with self study was felt even more strongly by some members who were committed to social action. "I feel like I'm being bought off," was the way one member put it.

Other members were not as angry, but they felt the tension between inward self-orientation and outward action. One very active parishioner stated her mixed feelings about where consultation fit into Dumbarton's priorities:

I see real progress in human relations and organization, but we haven't changed the character of the congregation toward social action. We have freed up money but when I see all the money put into consultation I wonder if it was worth it. We could have spent it on something else.

The planning and evaluation committee also went to the congregation for their ideas and opinions. Fifty-six members responded to a detailed survey with high satisfaction in worship (96%). Strong satisfaction was expressed (in declining order) for the community life, the Community Life Sunday, Administrative Board actions, and finances (from 80% through 73%). More than half were satisfied with adult education (61%) and religious education for children (55%), but only one-third were satisfied with the social action program (32%). Fellowship was the most appreciated part of Dumbarton's life in 1972; and involvement and commitment to the church were the qualities seen as most lacking and most needing emphasis in 1973.

COMMUNICATION PROBLEMS

The third area of responsibility for the planning and

evaluation committee concerned the work of the consultant. Larry Ulrich reported to the committee on the use
of his time. Dumbarton had contracted for ten and one-
half work days of Ulrich's time. Funds had been secured
for that amount. In early May, the consultant reported that
he had already worked the days for which he had been
contracted and needed two and one-half more days. One
committee member commented on this problem:

Larry used up almost all of his time and did not tell us
until it was used up. At that point we could not stop. The
board was reluctant to go on with the consultation and we
stopped inviting him to the meetings. Larry never gave us a
report of his time in writing and therefore he had not been
paid as of October, 1972. He didn't give us a running tally, but
would discuss figures in a loose sort of way. He should have
given us a monthly statement and a planned schedule we could
look at.

Ulrich's understanding of the financial argeement and
accounting was different from the committee's. He explained his perspective:

At the beginning of contract negotiations I told the committee
that I would need twelve and one-half days. They only had
money for ten days and I went in with the understanding that
if I needed more time, they would get more money. I gave
them an account at every meeting, though not in writing. The
committee regularly decided where my time would go. I
thought I was accountable, but I know now that I should have
given a regular written statement.

This misunderstanding between Ulrich and the planning
and evaluation committee points out how quickly communication can become tangled. Each party has its own
understanding and interpretation of what went on and
each party believes that its view is correct. When negotiat-

ing contracts, no one can ever assume that communications are clear. It is important to clarify and then re-clarify agreements.

The committee had another problem with Ulrich after the consultation had been completed. He had promised Dumbarton a documented report in early June but he moved out of town and did not get it to Dumbarton until early October, four months later, thus delaying the final report of the planning and evaluation committee. Members were angry, feeling that a lot of their impetus had worn off because of Ulrich's delay.

Still others felt that though they had benefited from the consultation, it had ended too abruptly. As one person put it:

There was no sending forth. I feel we need to crystallize our accomplishments. We needed a statement such as, "Here's where we go from here."

FINAL EVENTS

After a year of very hard work, the Administrative Board held its annual retreat in May, 1972, to review the year and plan for the future. It was a particularly significant retreat since it represented the culmination of a long year's work with consultative help. Fifteen board members attended, along with the pastor and the consultant. The board's major attention was given to reviewing the committees' progress reports and the congregational survey. They divided into three work groups to look at problems and recommend alternatives. On Saturday afternoon each of the three groups presented its report to the total group so that the board could set policies. In a brief summary the board made the following recommendations to the congregation:

(1) The commission on social concerns was to function as an enabling commission for overall support of various opinions and concerns. Rather than act as the congregation's conscience, the commission depended on the members to take initiative.

(2) The education committee called for a long-range planning session for the next year and for emphasis on adult education.

(3) The finance committee was to develop a five-year projection of the church's priorities in terms of work and money.

Harry Kiely explained the importance of the board's recommendations for the congregation:

The board thrashed out a position statement on several issues for our congregation. For example, they took a position on social action—an issue they had previously dodged. They received so much input from the congregation in terms of reports and representatives that what comes out in the policy statement is very much a representation of what the congregation is asking for.

A member of the commission on social concerns also commented on his sense of involvement: "I do feel involved in decisions and I do feel I have a say. People don't get pushed out."

The Administrative Board also heard a presentation by the pastor-parish relations committee. The board adopted "in principle" the Pastoral Role Definition, noting that further work needed to be done. This document included four major items: compensation, working conditions, pastoral responsibilities, and an evaluation. They concluded their retreat by conducting an extensive evaluation of the consultation, both oral and written.

EVALUATION OF THE CONSULTATION

At the board retreat, members expressed the highest degree of satisfaction with the work done on defining the pastor's role. They were also very pleased with the fall parish planning conference and the follow-up to it. Though the board did not keep in touch with the planning and evaluation committee, it expressed a general satisfaction with the committee's work and expressed a desire for a closer connection between the board and the committees. A high degree of satisfaction was felt about the functioning of the consultant, especially for his ability in gathering and facilitating the flow of information in the parish. The greatest dissatisfaction was that because he worked so exclusively with the board and its committees, so little of Ulrich's work touched the general congregational membership.

After the evaluation, Larry Ulrich presented to the board an analysis of the consultation from his point of view. He reviewed the major areas covered—pastor-parish relations, parish planning and goal-setting, and evaluation. Ulrich recommended that quarterly reports from the pastor and semi-annual reports from the board should give the congregation a clear picture of what is and is not being done. He also recommended that congregational survey results be put in an organized and useful form. He did not recommend further consultation at that time.

Although the consultation was completed at the board retreat in May, both Harry Kiely and the planning and evaluation committee evaluated the consultation from their unique points of view. Kiely, in a written evaluation, made several observations in areas other than those already mentioned. He noted:

Ulrich allowed us to be ourselves, to shape our own life and mission without imposing goals or structures on us. He could cut through a tangle of conversation and enable us to see the issues we were struggling with. He also provided helpful pressure by holding us to the goals we had set. As for myself, he helped me to affirm my strengths and be more aware of my weaknesses and see what I might do about them.

Kiely went on to note several ways in which the consultation might have been more helpful:

I felt the instrument used to gather data about pastoral expectations was inadequate. The importance of some pastoral functions cannot be measured by hours invested.

There was too little awareness of the consultant's work here on the part of the congregation, and hence few appreciate his contribution. It is doubtless a compliment to Larry that we felt that "We did it ourselves." Yet I think there needs to be an appreciation of the fact that we did indeed receive help and what the nature of that help was. Larry accentuated our strengths and not our weaknesses. Though I am for building on strengths, I also feel we could learn and grow by looking at our weaknesses.

The planning and evaluation committee also worked up a written report on the consultation in October, 1972. Its approach was slightly different and addressed itself to the following question: Where are we today as a result of the consultation in comparison with where we would have been if we had not become involved in it? The committee came to the conclusion that the congregation as a whole had adopted a futuristic approach to planning, rather than the hand-to-mouth system which had been the type of planning prior to the consultation. The definition of the pastor's role was perhaps the first document of that kind in the Baltimore Conference of the Methodist Church. A good start has been made toward including self-evaluation as part of the normal operation at Dumbarton. The church has developed strong leadership in its members and has also increased the number of individuals who are actively involved.

The planning and evaluation committee concluded its report by noting the consultant's reluctance to deal with confrontation. The committee felt that there were numerous times when obvious differences occurred and Larry Ulrich pushed for agreement rather than deal with the differences. Bob Gell, several months after the consultation, explained the long-range implications of conflict. "Our differences are just as much with us now as before. Recently we have found that there is more disunion and disharmony at Dumbarton than ever!"

Finally, the committee reported appreciation for the consultation and noted some skepticism. While many felt an unbiased, disinterested adviser was helpful in giving feedback and facilitating the work of the groups, other members felt consultative assistance should be limited so as to avoid unhealthy dependence on outside help.

Several months later, members reflected on the consultant's effectiveness. Some felt that Larry Ulrich had helped them see themselves more clearly. They remembered his amazing perception concerning what people said. Now committees were able to get at their questions more easily and work more efficiently to break down large jobs and get the work done. One person stated the ongoing learnings for the church as a whole. "Consultation helped us get on the track in a minimum amount of time, and that process did not end when Larry left."

Although Dumbarton church has developed a strong sense of community, some members raised questions about their unique Christian identity. Dumbarton has questioned its reason for being and its overall purpose. It has asked why it does what it does, but it has not resolved the question. Now that the pastor's role has been clarified, the congregation sees its next job as discovering and working out the role of members. Perhaps this will overcome a general sense that Dumbarton church lacks a firm idea of itself. Many members wistfully note that the consultation did not help them discover their unique Christian identity. They point out that they did not ask questions like that, so the issue was not addressed. It is an issue that is high on their agenda for next year.

ISSUES AND LEARNINGS

1 THE UNIQUENESS OF A SMALL CHURCH—Dumbarton church has one hundred members and forty pre-teen children. While the building is very large, the congregation is relatively small. Though the average pledge is higher than the national average, money is often scarce. But Dumbarton, being a small group, has developed a strong sense of community. People are drawn to the church by the feelings of intimacy and concern. Even those members who criticize the community are very active and continue to come. Because of the sense of community and involvement with each other, members give an unusual amount of time and energy to the church. Dumbarton has a very sophisticated organizational structure which includes many boards and a great deal of commitment. Individual members serve on several committees and give many hours of their time. Though there are difficulties, these people continue to come and give of themselves. They do all of the janitorial work, serve on committees, teach classes, and gather together on Sunday. A committee member would need a very good reason to miss church on Sunday. As one person put it, "I'd miss too much."

2 THE PASTOR IS CENTRAL TO ANY CHANGE EFFORTS—At Dumbarton every major effort to change has been supported and often stimulated by the pastor. When Harry Kiely arrived in 1968, the congregation was made up of a handful of people, most of them retired. Through Kiely's leadership, the membership and the character of the congregation changed to a young, family-oriented and worship-centered church. Harry Kiely introduced the idea of consultation, and the Administrative Board actually hired the consultant. The pastor was on board and involved in every way. Without his active participation, the consultation would never have gotten off the ground. While he has not been totally responsible for the changes, it is fair to say that unless Kiely works strongly for changes they do not get made.

3 DEALING WITH CONFLICT AND POLARIZATION—Dumbarton has been through many difficult crises where members experienced great conflict and polarization. The memory of these hard times remains painful to parishioners today. It is very difficult for a small congregation to deal with strong differences of opinion and conflicting interests in a constructive way. The tension between personal growth and social action at Dumbarton has caused severe polarization at times. The fall retreat of 1970 turned into a showdown between the two factions. Though personal growth "won," the entire congregation "lost" and suffered from the polarization. Through the use of an outside consultant Dumbarton learned to express its differences and work things out to the satisfaction of both sides. While the issue of social action vs. personal growth has never been fully resolved, the tension has provided Dumbarton with new opportunities for growth and greater communication.

4 IMPORTANCE OF AN OUTSIDE CONSULTANT—Consultant Larry Ulrich was able to provide a different perspective for Dumbarton church because he was an outside party. He was particularly helpful to the pastor in clarifying his role in the parish and supporting his effort to change. The consultant was also instrumental in planning and leading the parish retreats. As an outsider who did not have the involvement and investment of active members, Ulrich could clarify communications, suggest new ways to deal with differences of opinion, and push for follow-up plans and action.

5 DIFFICULTY OF CHANGING PARISH NORMS—With the use of consultation Dumbarton church went through a detailed process of gathering information from members, setting goals, working on ways to implement these goals, and finally evaluating the results. During the consultation and shortly after it had been completed, Dumbarton felt that growth and changes were taking place. As long as outside stimulus was provided by the consultant, the congregation continued to move ahead. In the six months since the consultation ended, Dumbarton has again experienced financial difficulties and conflict over interests and priorities. The congregation is now questioning how deeply the consultation affected its patterns of behavior. Some members wonder if parish norms were really changed. Some feel that the parish was lulled into a false sense of security. Dumbarton, like all parishes, is a complex organization with many assumed standards and relationships. Their present questions illustrate how complex and difficult it is for a congregation, as a group of people, to change their established norms.

CONCLUSION

The story of Dumbarton tells a lot about what it means to be a healthy parish in today's world. Dumbarton church is not a congregation free from conflict, controversy, or difficult times. There is a continuing tension at Dumbarton between differing points of view, although opinions are allowed to be expressed. There is also tension because people at Dumbarton have invested a lot in their congregation and they are honest, often ruthlessly honest, with themselves.

Dumbarton shows a sign of health in its ability to identify its needs as a parish and then use its external and internal resources to meet those needs. The parish has discovered and developed a structure in which change and growth are not just possibilities but a way of life. It is not easy for a group of people to grow together. Communication is broad and open; therefore, there are no great discrepancies in the way members see their church and in the events that took place in its history. These ingredients—honesty, community, accountability, openness, ability to identify and meet needs—all make up the unique mix which is Dumbarton church and point to a way of life that is both productive and satisfying for its members.

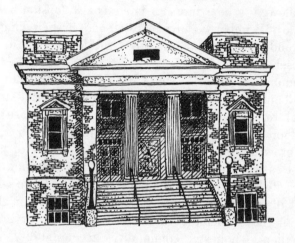

# 4

# THE STORY OF ALL SOULS'
# PRESBYTERIAN CHURCH

## BACKGROUND—AN INTERRACIAL CHURCH
## IN A CHANGING NEIGHBORHOOD

All Souls' Presbyterian Church is a congregation that is living out the meaning of change. Its actual creation as a church grew out of a need for change. Its setting has been a changing neighborhood, and its present life reflects the changes which formed its past history. Though change has been a constant ingredient in All Souls' life, it has taken many different forms.

After World War II, the north side of Richmond, Virginia, became a changing neighborhood. Blacks, seeking better housing, began moving into the mostly white north side. In turn, white families began moving out to the suburbs. While there was a serious depletion of white congregations, there was a strong need for black congregations. Realizing the changing need, the Hanover Presbytery of the Presbyterian Church, U.S., developed a plan to serve the new residents.

In 1947 and 1951, community surveys were taken and individuals were interviewed. The purpose of the surveys was to determine if a Presbyterian church should be started in the community. The church's concern, as described in a Presbytery report, would be:

. . . meeting the needs of the community in every aspect of life, on a basis of black-white cooperation, with the idea of pushing the black leadership to the front; that from this source we might also reach out to the underprivileged areas of the city.

Both black and white Christians expressed a desire for a broad kind of ministry. There was little enthusiasm for just another black congregation to be established by the Hanover Presbytery, but there was a real concern to establish an interracial open congregation that would provide a deepened and enriched kind of church life.

All Souls' Church was officially organized in December 1952. The Rev. Irvin Ellegan, a black Presbyterian minister, became the first pastor for the 48 charter members. For several years, services were held in the local elementary school, with various church meetings held at the manse and in the homes of members. A few years later the all-white Overbrook Presbyterian Church moved to a new location because of the changing neighborhood and All Souls' Church purchased its building.

All Souls is the first interracial Presbyterian church on the north side. During its early years, it was almost totally made up of black members, many of whom came from other denominations. There were two white, single members but no white families. All Souls also had a number of white students from Union Theological Seminary and the Presbyterian School of Christian Education who visited the church but who were not formal members. Until 1971, with the exception of the present pastor, All Souls had never had a white member serve on the Session.

Today All Souls' congregation is made up of a large number of middle class, professional, and white-collar members. In church attendance women outnumber men six to one. The present congregation of approximately 275 members is 85 percent black and 15 percent white.

All Souls reached its peak as a church in the '60s, with activity within the church and with an outward thrust into the community. Church programs flourished—the Every Member Canvass, Christian education with leadership training for teachers, Scouts, the day care center, and youth. A friend of All Souls, who was a neighborhood youth in the '60s, remembers the church as reaching out into the neighborhood:

All Souls has touched me. This church allowed me to go to my own church on Sundays and yet come here to the youth group. It was wonderful! There was something different to do every time.

Besides youth work, All Souls was socially active, reaching out into the community with voter registration drives and community meetings where political issues were thrashed out. When the Civil Rights Act was passed in 1964, the church held lengthy discussions about what members could do. A significant number of parishioners from All Souls picketed at lunch counters. Many members were active in community and city affairs, such as the Richmond Council on Human Relations and other civic and political groups. Many present members feel that what went on in the church helped people move out into the community.

In 1963 All Souls' first pastor left the church to work for the Division of Christian Action for the Presbyterian Church, U.S. A committee was formed to seek a new pastor, and it established new criteria for the new pastor:

he was to be black, have a strong pastoral ministry, and be a good preacher. After investigating several candidates, the committee dropped the criteria of race and concentrated on a strong pastoral ministry and preaching as criteria. In 1964 All Souls called the Rev. James G. Carpenter to be its pastor. Jim Carpenter, a white Presbyterian minister, was quite different from the former pastor.

Two major differences are noted by present parishioners of All Souls. While Ellegan regularly visited families in their homes, Carpenter did not. His style as moderator of the Session is very different from Ellegan's. Carpenter does not see his job as calling on subcommittees of the Session to make reports. Ellegan took initiative and asked for reports, keeping abreast of what was happening. Some members of the Session describe Carpenter's style as passive. Lay people have to take initiative and responsibility. If members need assistance on a project, they must seek it out, and Carpenter willingly provides his help. Carpenter also developed a strong ministry to the city of Richmond. At present he is serving his second term on the city council, being elected by a large black vote and receiving the third highest number of votes of all candidates. Although the Session officially approved Carpenter's running for office, as time went on certain members began to resent the amount of time he spent on city council affairs. One person noted:

The church is neglected and on the decline. All Souls is Jim's livelihood and it should have his full consideration.

Others see Carpenter's position as part of the real ministry of All Souls to the city of Richmond. One person put it this way:

I see Jim's council seat as part of our mission. I'm happy to give up my home visit so that he can have time to spend on city council, doing things that I cannot do.

QUESTIONS OF IDENTITY

By 1969, five years after Jim Carpenter's arrival, All Souls had experienced a gradual change in congregational life. The congregation was uncertain about who it was and where it was going. Although there was no severe conflict or crisis, All Souls was experiencing a general feeling of frustration and discontent on many levels. All Souls' programs were changing. When Carpenter first arrived, the church had already begun to move into a transition period. The men's group was dead, but had not officially disbanded. The women's circle had little participation. Though the church school was active at the beginning of Carpenter's ministry, by 1969 it was fading out. Children were not coming and teachers were frustrated. People were longing for the good old days. They were asking such questions as: "Who are we? Where are we going? Where are our life signs?" And they were not getting any answers.

Another factor was that more white people had joined the church. Still another was that the interracial tension being experienced in the church at that time was not being dealt with constructively. Though there had been a series of open church discussions, some members believed these to be superficial.

In 1973, there are a variety of opinions about All Souls' interracial tension. Some members do not recognize any tension between blacks and whites. Others say that if Carpenter left, most of the whites would also leave. One white member commented that she feels some black members are suspicious of whites. She has experienced an unwillingness by some blacks to engage in in-depth interaction. A black member noted interracial tension at Session meetings. He feels whites have been condescending when giving reports. The pastor observes that whites have different needs than blacks at All Souls; whites would really like to have in-depth contact across racial lines. Blacks do not seem to have these kinds of needs.

Jim Carpenter, as pastor of All Souls, was also discontented. As he remembers:

I was at the height of my frustration and ready to say goodbye to the church. We had reached a point where I saw little vitality and felt the best thing for me to do was exit. I felt part of the problem could be me. It was more of a mood of stagnation. There was no sense of direction and purpose and I felt inadequate to move beyond where we were.

In November of 1969 the elders and deacons of All Souls met together for a joint officers' meeting. Realizing that the church no longer had a sense of identity, the Session established a task force to study the purpose and programs of All Souls in order to clarify its identity. At the suggestion of a parishioner, Jim Carpenter contacted the Rev. Irving Stubbs of TRUST, Inc., a consulting firm with church affiliations in Richmond. Carpenter shared with consultant Stubbs the church's situation and together they developed some guidelines for choosing the task force. These included inviting a cross section of members—black and white, male and female, liberal and conservative—and attempting to come up with a group that would be open to new directions.

One month later, the Session approved the self-study and guidelines, and it appointed members of the task force. Since the task force did not include any Session members it was to report its findings to the Session.

Jim Carpenter recalls his own difficulties in working with the Session during this period:

Although I got along well with members of the Session on an individual basis, I did not know how to find constructive ways for the total body to accomplish tasks. I was aware of a lot of ferment and believed that could be a positive force. Yet, I felt a need to by-pass the Session and establish a task force. The Session was not very open and was not able to look inward. Its members were older people who thought alike. I felt we needed a structure that more adequately reflected the diversity of the membership.

## CLARIFYING PARISH IDENTITY

Earlier in 1970 All Souls' task force, with Jim Carpenter as chairman, began diligently working to clarify All Souls' identity. The total group numbered 16, but the nucleus of active members was only 8. They met weekly and for three Sundays administered surveys to the congregation and visitors. Another input into the study was the task force's own ideas and feelings. Members were able to move beyond the superficial level and share deeply with each other. After nine months of study, the task force developed a position statement on All Souls' identity. It was able to clarify "who they were" and "who they wanted to be," yet the task force was unable to figure out "how to get there." For several months, the task force foundered, not knowing what to do with all of the data it had gathered. Finally, Carpenter stopped calling any meetings. He noted:

I was frustrated. They were frustrated. And I didn't know what to do. I had skills in group dynamics and pastoral counseling but not in planning and getting tasks done. I spent a great deal of time reflecting feelings, making people feel good, but there was little sense of direction. We were spinning our wheels.

In December 1970, Jim Carpenter again called Irving Stubbs and discussed the task force's problems. Stubbs attended a meeting of the task force and afterwards shared with them what he observed. He clearly saw the high frustration level. He noted that the group was made up of several very sharp, bright professionals, but it was running dry. "You can't reflect on feelings and data forever," he told them. The group did not know how to direct its research into any action plans.

Another problem of the task force concerned the report to the Session. With no member of the Session on the task force, the group was afraid the report might not be accepted. For example, one idea of the task force was to have free dialogue instead of a sermon and to try freer forms of worship. Members felt a need to bring the Session up to date on where they were. Irving Stubbs suggested that the form of the report would affect the Session's response. The task force needed to give the Session several different options rather than one definite proposal. The options focused on setting clear goals for All Souls. Irving Stubbs was suggested as a consultant for this process. Specific options included:

(1) An officers' retreat.
(2) Goal-setting for officers and congregation.
(3) A congregational meeting.
(4) A life-planning lab.

## BRINGING THE OFFICERS ON BOARD

After establishing these alternatives, the task force submitted its report to the Session and disbanded. Two members of the task force attended a joint officers' meeting of the Session and the board of deacons to present the report and get input from them. The Session accepted the report and had little to add to it. It had been prepared by a cross section of the congregation with a great deal of input from members, and it was an accurate reflection of the ideas of all the members. The Session then discussed the specific options that were proposed.

There was a mixed response to the use of a consultant. Some members of the Session, fearing the unknown, were reluctant about it, even though All Souls did not have to pay any money. The Hanover Presbytery had provided funds to support TRUST, Inc. and TRUST had a contract to provide services to local churches. In order to overcome the resistance, the officers examined the different roles a consultant might play. He would help All Souls set its own goals; he would not set the goals himself. He possessed unique skills as an enabler, and could help members become involved and do the work themselves. Working developmentally was crucial. First the officers could learn to set their own personal goals and then move on to church goals. After two meetings, the officers voted to have an officers' retreat with a life-planning lab, and then to move to congregational goal-setting. Dates were set for both events.

### OFFICERS' RETREAT BUILDS TRUST

In order to begin the goal-setting process, the officers of All Souls gathered at Camp Hanover for a weekend retreat. Several of their spouses attended, making a total of 16 participants. Irving Stubbs served as the consultant leader, with Jim Carpenter attending as a participant. The focus of the retreat was to help individuals learn to set goals for their lives and then move on to begin setting goals for the church.

The officers' group began on Saturday morning, April 24, 1971. Several officers remember coming to that weekend with excitement and apprehension. No one had ever participated in any training in planning before. This was a first for All Souls. The group began by drawing a life line and fantasizing about the future. Afterwards members learned to transform their fantasies into goals and then share them with others. They ended by learning how to use a force-field analysis. Members found this technique particularly helpful in determining ways to reach a goal. As one person explained:

My wife and I have been married over ten years and she has never been to visit her family in the Midwest. Life-planning helped us figure out a way to make that trip possible. We were able to identify and overcome the factors that kept my wife from making the trip.

The life-planning lab, while very personal, was also very practical. Members found the experience immediately applicable to their lives. They were also moving from new terms, like goal-setting, to reality. Now people understood from experience what those strange words meant. They also had the experience of working with a consultant and moving into a futuristic stance.

On Sunday the officers came back together to begin plans for setting goals for All Souls. The officers hammered out objectives for the goal-setting process. Included in the objectives were the following:

(1) to establish a church that would make Christ meaningful and enable us to serve our fellowman;

(2) to enable officers to provide positive leadership;

(3) to cultivate an environment conducive to growth and ministry;

(4) to have a systematic method of planning, executing tasks, and evaluating.

A work group composed of officers was set up to carry out the general design and details for the congregational meeting. The group carefully worked out a calendar for the upcoming events.

Besides the life-planning lab and goal-setting work, the officers' weekend accomplished several other significant things. Though lack of trust had not been an obvious characteristic of officers' meetings, the trust level had been low. During this retreat, they grew to trust and depend on each other. Changes were coming for All Souls. The officers had put themselves on the line by freely sharing their power with the congregation.

Many participants attributed the increase in trust to consultant Irving Stubbs. As one person remarked:

Irving Stubbs invites trust. He has a tremendous gift for helping people open up and begin to think in new ways. He has freedom to share and help others share.

Jim Carpenter remembers that initially he was aggravated by the idea of seeking outside help and that before he got to know Stubbs he had basically negative feelings about TRUST, Inc. After Stubbs met with the task force in 1970, and after the officers' retreat, Carpenter changed his mind:

I did not feel threatened by Irving. He never took over at all. I had full freedom. It was freeing to see someone who had skills in planning and goal setting that I didn't have. Irving demonstrates care and concern for people and can enable folk to move beyond where they were. Some of my ego needs were met by his presence.

Carpenter, instead of leading the retreat, had an opportunity to participate like everyone else. He later commented that his equal position made him feel more human than he had ever felt before with the officers. By Stubbs's example, Jim Carpenter also learned new ways to handle conflict. One participant was expressing strong hostility and resistance during the retreat. Irving Stubbs was able to convey to the officer that he heard him and was for him but that the group had a task to do and was going to do it. Carpenter learned from Stubbs that one could deal with conflict and also get things done.

Learning to trust each other, to plan ahead, to develop realistic goals, to deal with conflict constructively, and still to get the job done—these were important movements for All Souls. Only when the officers and the pastor —the people who make the decisions—had begun to learn these skills did the rest of All Souls move ahead. All Souls was no longer spinning its wheels. The church had taken a major step on the way to securing awareness of its identity.

CONGREGATION SETS PRIORITIES

Sunday, May 16, 1971, turned out to be a milestone event in the life of All Souls. The work group established at the officers' retreat had designed the all-day congregational meeting and notified people through calls, letters, and announcements. Ninety out of 300 members arrived bright and early at Virginia Union University, a large, black, Baptist university in Richmond. This was a large turn-out for All Souls, since the usual attendance at congregational meetings averaged 35 people.

After a short devotional service, Jim Carpenter began by giving the history of how All Souls had come to this point. He spoke of the frustrations of the late '60s and told of the work of the original task force, going on to explain Irving Stubbs's role as consultant. He concluded with a review of the joint officers' retreat, leading up to this day with the entire congregation.

After everyone had been brought up to date, Irving Stubbs shared with the group the statement developed by the original task force and then refined by the Session and joint officers.

### "WHO ARE WE?"
(How Do We See Ourselves?)

We are persons belonging to a group that is trying to be Christian. We see ourselves primarily in terms of the interpersonal relationships *within* All Souls. Our top priority as a congregation centers in worship. Here we sometimes have meaningful worship, and we both want and resist change in worship forms. We are blacks and whites in equality, and yet we are unsure what it means to be an interracial congregation. Are we black, black and white, white and black? Are we Presbyterian, a black congregation, an integrated congregation, or a black congregation open to whites? We lack both ongoing personal contact and joint community service across racial lines. We have identity with a body of Christians, a community that is aware of community problems and yet not geared to deal with them. In All Souls we have an openness, an honesty in trying to deal with ourselves, our faith and the world, and yet little chance for real communication. We belong to a fellowship willing to be self-critical and yet we get anxious when criticism takes place. All Souls offers us some security in that it is a regular place to worship; a place of spiritual reinforcement; we have some roots here.

We experience among ourselves friendship and fellowship —and yet we are frustrated because our friendship and fellowship are not deeper and broader. We lack a visible concern and love for our fellowship members: elderly, lonely, and sick. We have differing views as to the role and method of operation of the pastor. Some like the way he operates; others do not.

We belong to a supportive community where we look at life with all of its different aspects. Here we seek a unity of life. We are not clear as to our purpose and to our future—individually, or as a congregation. Yet, here we are helped to define our role as Christians.

All participants were given a copy of the statement before they broke into small groups to give their input. They were asked to discuss the question: "Is this how we see ourselves?" When the groups shared their reactions, they found an amazing agreement about the identity statement. It truly reflected the opinions of the entire congregation. The answer to the question was "yes." The members discussed whether or not they agreed with the statement on "Who We Want To Be." The response again was "Yes."

The group then moved on to set priorities for the goals of All Souls. Each person was given a sheet of 61 possible goals, drawn up from the previous data by Jim Carpenter and a seminarian. Everyone was also given 100 points to distribute to the goals of his or her highest priority. Space was also provided for adding other goals and making comments. Since the raw data produced was so extensive, it was turned over to the work group to collate, analyze, and turn into a report to the congregation and the Session later in the year.

One of the ongoing questions of identity for All Souls had to do with the ratio of blacks to whites. There was a growing fear among some members that All Souls was becoming a white congregation. Irving Stubbs was able to help the group begin to come to terms with this question through a perception test. He said, "Let's see what you think about the percentage of blacks to whites." After polling the members, Stubbs shared with them the actual figures. The result showed that people thought there were more whites than there actually were. One possible explanation for the mistake was that whites, being in the minority, were more visible than blacks. This quick check was another way for members to clarify a factor in their identity.

Irving Stubbs concluded the conference with his own comments about the groups' work and then asked the total group to discuss what had gone on. Most members felt very positive about the event, realizing that a great number of people had spoken very frankly. A few were uncomfortable because they had come from backgrounds where the pastor directly led the flock. They were not used to having a significant input and becoming involved. Some preferred not to be involved. As for Jim Carpenter, he felt very encouraged. He thought that it was one of the most productive experiences he had had in the church.

This all-day congregational meeting was crucial to the change efforts at All Souls. It was the one time a large percentage of the members came together to make corporate plans for their church. Not only could they acknowledge the work done so far, but they also had an opportunity to contribute to future plans. The planning and decision-making was no longer solely the prerogative of the pastor and the officers. The congregation was brought on board and was involved.

### ANALYZING THE CONGREGATION'S INPUT

The information on All Souls had been gathered, yet the job of organizing and making sense out of the data remained to be done. Immediately after the congregational meeting, the work group met weekly to collate the raw material, put it in some understandable form, and report back to the congregation. This effort took many hours of hard work. As one member put it, "We had forty meetings of ten hours each. The chairman would not let us go until midnight."

Out of this massive amount of material came 66 goals which were mailed to the congregation and discussed at a Sunday morning meeting. The congregation accepted the analysis, and no major revisions were made. For the first 16 goals there was an absolute positive correlation between the total number of persons who voted. For example, goal #1—to have both traditional and innovative worship services—got the highest number of votes (533). (The 100 points could be divided any way the voter wished.) More people (49) voted for it than any other item.

A 100 percent positive correlation suggests that the system of priority-making was faulty. Although the possible goals were placed at random on the individual scoring sheets, it turned out that the ones that came first on the page got the top priority. This suggests that people were throwing points to the early options. Another afterthought was that if a member added new goals or comments on his paper, other people did not have an opportunity to see them.

At this point the work group's job had just begun. Now, what to do with these 66 goals? Before making recommendations to the Session, the work group divided into subgroups to develop action steps and make recommendations. These ideas went back and forth between the subgroup and the large work group three times before being finalized. One member described this experience:

My subgroup would develop a recommendation and the total group would butcher it. They'd say we had done an overkill or gone too far. Everybody really learned to fight for his or her position. It was rough but we learned not to rubber-stamp ideas.

Finally, in July, the work group presented a report to the Session recommending that 16 of the 66 goals be implemented and that major emphasis be given to the first four ranked goals. These concerned worship, Christian education, developing a pastoral ministry team, and bringing in families with varied economic background. Along with these goals were suggestions for specific action steps to implement the goals. The Session studied the work group's report carefully. It made several revisions and added its own input. It accepted the 16 goals and farmed out 9 of them to existing committees for implementation. There appeared to be good, free interplay between the work group and the Session.

During this implementation period, Irving Stubbs, the chairman of the work group, and Jim Carpenter regularly assessed what was going on. Stubbs had suggested five goals, but as one person put it, "We got all fired up and took on 16." This proved to be too many. Certain committees were given too many tasks and never given a date to complete their work.

Looking back to that early summer of 1971 members of the work group recall their different feelings:

The highest point was the work group's sense of dedication to following through. I don't see how in the world the chairman held that group together.

Another commented:

The process was very tiring. We picked too many goals and loaded everybody down. I felt cheated because not a great deal was accomplished. I don't know, but I doubt I'd do it again.

Still another was angry because none of the top 16 had to do with outreach. This person saw that the lack of goals on mission was a true reflection of the priorities at All Souls. (The only outreach is in the form of benevolences and the pastor's position on city council.) "A lot of people think this is a gung ho church because it's interracial. I was shocked because it's just another middle class church. Changes come so slowly here."

PASTOR AND OFFICERS WORK ON ROLES

As the change efforts at All Souls had shifted leadership and authority from the pastor to the officers and then to the congregation, this distribution of power had also raised questions about the pastor's and officers' roles. In the midsummer of 1971, the Session began to seek clarity about the function of the pastor. Carpenter was white, political, and a spontaneous sort of person. Some officers felt the pastor was not pushing people enough while others saw real value in shared leadership. The pastor himself was raising questions about his role.

The officers and pastor went through a process of management by objectives. Stubbs, reflecting back, opposed a job description because it might prove limiting and could set strict boundaries on people. As he put it, "If people can develop goals and objectives for a job, then they may see their job in terms of opportunities instead of limits. Management by objectives also gives people a way to measure their work."

On a Sunday afternoon and evening in August, 1971 the officers and Carpenter met together with Stubbs serving as a leader-consultant. Each person developed individual goals, zeroing in on what he or she wanted to accomplish as an officer for the coming year. Jim Carpenter did the same thing, developing a clear statement on what he wanted to accomplish as pastor. Officers helped each other define goals. As a total group the participants made plans to follow up and check on this process toward objectives. Carpenter would meet with groups of three every six months to go over each other's progress and work. This not only provided a way for the officers and the pastor to keep in touch, but it also gave them a supportive structure to work on their goals and their individual roles.

A NEW CHURCH SEASON BRINGS MORE CHANGES

The church year, from fall 1971 to summer 1972, was filled with many different experiences for All Souls. Members were clearer about who they were as a church. Everyone was aware of the 16 major goals set by the congregation and committees were trying to implement them. Many were finding this a difficult job. Some members remember a vague sense of disappointment because not all of the 16 goals were being met. One example was the committee for a monthly newsletter. One member noted, "We'd get the action steps together, but every time it came to getting a person to do them, the newsletter fell apart."

One major accomplishment had to do with worship. This project, assumed by the work group, was to present a variety of options for worship. Members planned and wrote four services during Advent. The congregation began to come closer together in its attitudes toward worship. Differences between innovative and traditional services did not appear to be so great.

Communication between church groups or individuals also seemed to be improving. As Carpenter put it, "I started getting more direct calls. Our level of communication is different now. It's deeper and more honest. We don't shake every time there is conflict."

Also in 1972 Carpenter worked on his own objectives

of developing skills in goal-setting. In February he attended a Lyle Schaller Training Laboratory in goal-
setting for organizations. In the early part of 1972 Carpenter became interested in the charismatic movement.
His wife had experienced the "baptism of the Holy Spirit"
and Carpenter began to study the charismatic movement
in an effort to understand his wife's experience. Later he
too received the "baptism of the Holy Spirit" and he
spoke in tongues. Carpenter seems caught between two
drives—one to avoid appearing pious when he speaks of
his new spiritual life and another feeling that his experience must be shared. He does not force it on others. He
feels God offers many gifts to people and speaking in
tongues is only one of them.

As for the officers of All Souls, by February 1972, they
were beginning to feel the overload of their work. More
and more joint officers' meetings were necessary to coor-
dinate changes and plans. A lot of reduplication was
taking place. A committee of the Session was set up to
study a more efficient way of operating. Officers found
that their church structure was getting in the way of
their efficiency and mission. By June the committee had
developed a tentative plan for merging the elders and the
deacons and using subcommittees to carry out the different responsibilities. All Souls began to change through
planning and goal-setting. As members became more
deeply involved and responsible, the climate changed and
finally structural changes were made to accommodate the
needs.


REFLECTIONS ON THE CONSULTATION

The church season of 1971–72 had brought new experiences and changes to All Souls. Though Jim Carpenter
and Irving Stubbs had kept in contact on a casual basis,

Stubbs did not work with All Souls in any major capacity. Looking back over his experience with the church, Irving Stubbs discussed his role:

My approach was more spontaneous than preconceived. Jim Carpenter is a highly competent minister and has a great ability to work internally; therefore, 60 percent of the consultative work was on Jim's part. I began with a clear contract for consultation in planning but after the goal-setting, my contract was not clear. My role shifted more to organization development consultation.

Jim Carpenter has also done a lot of reflection on All Souls' consultation experience. In an oral case study to seminarians at Union Theological Seminary in Richmond, Carpenter described the value of using a consultant:

At first I thought a consultant would make me insecure but actually I felt *more* secure. I could not have made the changes by myself. A third party is neutral. His self-interests are different. Irving didn't have the blind spots since he wasn't as close to the system as the rest of us. I feel it's essential to have a third party because it puts the pastor in a different role and opens people up to think in a new way. As far as the Church is concerned, it needs to have the capacity to hang loose and want to change. It needs to assume that people are capable of growing and doing things for themselves.

Some members question the value of their consultation experience. The overall mood at All Souls is one of fatigue and frustration. Many members who were very active and involved in the consultation feel depleted. They do not see any results or changes from their long, hard work. As one member put it:

After all the work has been done, we have not made any progress. Even though we have set goals, we still have the same sense of frustration. With the possible exception of the Session's work together, I can't see any changes. We aren't doing anything that we did not do prior to the consultation.*

## ISSUES AND LEARNINGS

1 CHANGE CAN TAKE PLACE WITHOUT TRAUMA. All Souls' need for change grew out of its general sense of frustration, lifelessness, and discontent. The church did not experience any earth-shattering crisis or trauma. All Souls engaged in consultation in a rather loose contractual way. The consultant had a low profile, while Carpenter provided much of the internal directions for change. The relationship between All Souls and Irving Stubbs was spontaneous. Stubbs was called in as a need arose. All Souls never became excessively dependent on Stubbs because the pastor and members assumed responsibility for the work and carried it out.

2 THE PASTOR CAN PROVIDE NECESSARY IMPETUS AND LEADERSHIP FOR CHANGE. Jim Carpenter is a highly competent pastor. He found that he welcomed a consultant's help rather than felt threatened by it. Carpenter has a great ability to work internally for changes and thus to provide a major part of the leadership and direction for All Souls' change effort. Consultant Irving Stubbs could work with Carpenter to see that changes were occurring. He did not always have to be personally involved and physically

---

* An interesting sidelight on the problem of closure in consultation is the fact that the consultant had no knowledge of the member's feelings expressed in this quote until the case history was actually researched and written. In this situation the consultation would have benefited from a more systematic review process between the consultant and the Session of All Souls. Also out of this experience it would seem important to provide for such a review process to continue at least one year beyond the formal consultative activity period.

present. Carpenter was able to learn skills from Irving Stubbs and also use him for guidance and analysis.

3 CHANGES OCCUR PROGRESSIVELY. At All Souls one change influenced and initiated another. The task force moved from a state of inaction to a point where they were able to give the Session specific proposals. The officers and pastor then experienced a growing level of trust and commitment to setting goals at the life-planning lab. Next, the entire congregation was asked to become involved. The climate appeared to be more hopeful and people became more honest with each other. After goals had become clearer, the officers and pastor worked on their roles by setting objectives. Finally, the officers realized that people were overworked and that their structure was overloaded and top heavy. In order to become more efficient, the board of deacons and the Session merged. An overview shows that changes first occurred in the way people related to each other and carried out tasks. These were followed by changes in the structure of All Souls.

4 RETREATS AND EVENTS AWAY FROM THE CHURCH BUILD-ING ARE MAJOR OPPORTUNITIES FOR CHANGE. All Souls was able to move forward every time the members spent time together away from the parish. The officers' weekend retreat at Camp Hanover started the goal-setting process. The entire congregation then spent the day at Virginia Union University to create priorities among the church's goals. Later the officers and pastor gathered for a Sunday afternoon and evening to work on their roles. These three experiences appear as significant events at which important changes in the consultation occurred at All Souls.

CONCLUSION

The story of All Souls' Church presents a picture of a variety of changes. Over a period of time, with a great deal of effort, All Souls could move from a frustrated position to set clearer goals for officers and the church. Often churches cannot move beyond setting goals. All Souls' experience shows how detailed, thorough action steps were developed. A breakdown occurred because of lack of initiation, motivation and follow-through, lack of adequate leadership training, and lack of an evaluation instrument. All Souls' story shows how one church attempted to clarify its identity and mission by concentrating on goals.

# 5

# THE STORY OF ST. JAMES' EPISCOPAL CHURCH

## THE CITY AND THE CHURCH

In the northeastern corner of Texas, bordering on Arkansas and approximately thirty miles from both Louisiana and Oklahoma, lies the city of Texarkana. Texarkana has a population of 52,000 and was named for three states —Texas, Arkansas, and Louisiana. On the main street of Texarkana, one block from the spacious city square, is St. James' Church. Most of the St. James parishioners live in Texarkana and are for the most part active citizens. There is no great contrast between life at St. James and life in Texarkana. St. James appropriately reflects the city's way of life, and in order to understand the parish, one needs to get the flavor of the city.

Parishioners and residents of Texarkana use the term "East Texas" to describe their section of the country. East Texas is more than a description of Texarkana's geographical location. It refers to a way of life that is commonly identified with the deep South. Residents in East Texas feel that their life style is more relaxed and more traditional than the western Texas style of life.

Texarkana is unique in that it is a border city. Located on the state line, it has 30,000 residents in Texas and 22,000 in Arkansas. This seems not to cause severe problems, although it takes longer to get municipal legislation passed because of the necessary approval by both states. Texarkana has two school systems, two police departments, two mayors, and two city councils, but one post office and one chamber of commerce. The major employer is the defense industry. Government installations support the Red River Army Depot and the Lone Star Army Ammunition Plant. Other sources of employment include some manufacturing and agriculture.

Race relations have been difficult for Texarkana. The city is 30 percent black, with no significant Mexican or Indian population. The ratio of blacks to whites is high for Texas, though low for East Texas. Though the Ku Klux Klan (KKK) was very powerful before World War II, it no longer exists. Some whites see real progress being made in race relations, while blacks in Texarkana claim that the supposed signs of racial progress are deceptive. Some changes have taken place, but the blacks question whether any significant progress has been made. They note that no blacks have ever been elected to public office; they have campaigned, however, and have been defeated. Socially there is little mixing between blacks and whites. In 1971 two black churches were burned to the ground. This shocked both the white and the black community. Some citizens believe arsonists were responsible, since the burnings took place shortly before election day and several black candidates attended these two churches. The white community responded financially and also gave volunteer support to help rebuild the churches. A year later no one had been arrested for the burnings.

Texarkana is not a strong church community. There are

149 churches, representing 25 denominations. Yet when the Kiwanis Club sponsors its annual Church Loyalty Sunday, only 15,000 citizens attend church, 29 percent of the city's population.

## ST. JAMES' EPISCOPAL CHURCH

St. James' Episcopal Church is well-known in Texarkana. From the wide downtown street, one immediately notices its pleasant physical plant. It includes an old, traditional church building with large red doors opening into the worship area, which has dark wooden pews and a pale blue wall behind the altar. The effect is one of warmth, solemnity, and peacefulness. In addition to the church building, St. James has a large parish hall used for church offices, church school on Sundays, and many community projects during the week. Over 6,000 community people use St. James' facilities each month for their projects. These include the senior citizens group, "meals on wheels," Weight Watchers, and the human relations council. The "meals on wheels" project, which uses St. James, was the first program of its type in the nation and has since become a model for others. St. James has provided "seed money" for some of the projects.

The larger of the two Episcopal churches in town, St. James has approximately 700 baptized members and 200 contributing individuals or families. Its annual budget is approximately $60,000. On an average Sunday, 300 people attend services. In recent years, St. James has had two or three parishioners enter the ministry each year—a record in the Diocese of Dallas.

St. James was the first white church to admit blacks, and it is seen as the "liberal" church in the community. At present there are twelve black communicants. Outsiders notice that certain parishioners are active in com-

munity projects, but the parishioners do not see their church as "liberal," socially active, or reaching out into the community to bring in blacks.

There appear to be several other discrepancies between the church's image in the community and its image within the parish. One very touchy question concerns exactly who goes to St. James. Some see St. James parishioners as important to the city's power structure, and make statements like, "The chamber of commerce goes to St. James." Others refer to St. James as the "country club set," declaring that more of its parishioners belong to the country club than of any other church in town. The rector, along with other leaders in the parish, sees this as a glaring exaggeration. In fact, he takes pride in the fact that if St. James was ever the country club set or the chamber of commerce church, that is specifically what it is not now.

Some newcomers who join the church find it difficult to be accepted. Several angrily commented, "If I weren't a strong Episcopalian, I wouldn't stay." Or, "This is my church, regardless of how I am treated, and no one will keep me out." Newcomers are very conscious of the cliques and established groups. They express wishes that more of their social needs could be met at church. Both newcomers and long-established parishioners have expressed a desire for a stronger sense of community within the parish. Yet many of the well-established members expect their social needs to be met at the country club rather than the church. Some come to church solely for religious needs. As one prominent parishioner explained: "I go to church here, but my social life is at the country club. Other people's social life is at the pool hall." Another specified his need: "I don't care about the church's image in the community—I'm going to come here to worship God. Sacraments are important to me."

Along with its image in the community and the difficulties of newcomers in feeling accepted, St. James has
several unwritten standards which perhaps point to the
fact that parishioners' social needs are met elsewhere. As
a rule parish meetings never run over two hours, and few
show up. Vestry meetings are held for one hour after
church on Sunday.

For the past ten years, the rector of St. James has been
an Episcopal priest named Richard C. Allen. Fr. Allen is
well-loved by his parishioners and very active in the
community. He is known all over town for his ecumenical
spirit, his liberal views, and his active social ministry.
Many refer to him as the "good Samaritan of Texarkana"
or *"the* social worker of Texarkana." Within the parish,
Allen is seen as a strong pastor, not as a businessman or
administrator. As one parishioner describes him:

Fr. Allen is a dedicated man. He is on call night and day—
more so than a doctor. He does more charitable things than
any other man in town. Other churches in town send their
transients to Fr. Allen. Over twenty people a day come in and
Fr. Allen feeds them, sits down to talk with them and even
keeps a file on every one of them. Sometimes I feel he doesn't
have time to take care of *us* because of the transients.

Along with his strong pastoral ministry and social activism, Allen places emphasis on sacramental worship,
especially Holy Communion.

St. James' Church balances the two forces that create
tension in the community—a pull toward security and
tradition and a need to change and move ahead. The
congregation has opened its building to the community
and has accepted black members, yet it has difficulty
welcoming newcomers and tends to leave social work to
the rector. In 1970 St. James looked at the issues of
planned change through parish consultation. St. James,

already influenced by the changing forces of life in the city, opened itself to outside change agents and risked what might happen.

## DEVELOPING A CLIENT

In the early part of 1970, St. James entered into a consulting relationship with Project Test Pattern, represented by consultants James MacAdam Willson and the Rev. Alfred E. Persons. Mac Willson is a Roman Catholic layman, professionally employed as a management consultant at the NASA Manned Spacecraft Center. Al Persons is an Episcopal priest in private practice as a consultant to churches and educational institutions. Both men live in Houston, Texas, and have had wide training in management theory, behavioral science, group work, and organization development, supplemented by a week of PTP-sponsored orientation to consulting in parishes.

Persons and Willson were asked by PTP to develop a consulting relationship in a parish and report to PTP on their experience and learnings. The Rev. Loren B. Mead, Director of PTP, initially visited the late Avery C. Mason, then Bishop of Dallas, and wrote to three parishes Bishop Mason had recommended. He explained the project on parish renewal and asked if the parishes were interested in participating. Persons and Willson also wrote letters to the parishes. Of the three parishes contacted, one responded—St. James, Texarkana. The Rev. Richard Allen of St. James wrote a long, full letter about the church, its problems, and its possibilities for change. Allen appeared open and excited. He also telephoned Al Persons, a close personal friend from their days in the Diocese of Oklahoma. Commenting on St. James' first contact with PTP, Allen remarks: "When the bishop nominated us, it felt good and we thought that we were open to renewal."

Together Dick Allen and Al Persons set up a preliminary visit to discuss PTP and the possibility of a consulting relationship. Since Al Persons was to be out of town for the month of April, Mac Willson made the first visit alone on April 25–26, 1970, rather than postpone it.

At the rectory in Texarkana, the Allens and Willson began to discuss a possible relationship between PTP and St. James. Willson reported that Dick Allen seemed eager to be involved in the PTP project but he did not know how interested the rest of the parish might be. He appeared to be very anxious for change to be introduced at St. James but he did not know how to go about it. Allen recalls his viewpoint at the time:

I saw PTP as a process of renewal—like a guy who has gone to confession and is trying to lead a new life. I saw Mac and Al as coming in to take a look at us and our mission—who we were and what we were doing. I also felt that I was too liberal and didn't fit here, but I loved this parish and this community. There wasn't any rumbling about my liberal ministry because of my strong pastoral ministry, but I didn't see the parish moving ahead.

After church on Sunday, April 26, Mac Willson attended his first dinner meeting with 15 couples chosen by the rector. With the liberal element strongly represented, these people included vestry representatives and other influential parishioners. Willson was introduced and explained Project Test Pattern, its goals and its means of attaining them. He also spoke of their relationship working together as a team with St. James. The parishioners asked what specific areas they would work in, and Willson replied that part of the process would be to define those areas where work was needed. There was also a discussion of finances, which were an immediate problem. Willson then left the room so the group could discuss comfortably whether they would make a recommendation to the vestry to go ahead with PTP. They so decided.

Reflecting on that initial meeting, Willson felt his first contact had gone well. He was somewhat disturbed that Persons was not there, and he felt the parish had not grasped the team's relationship. "Five to fifteen thousand dollars for consultation is a stiff price," said Willson, "but they seemed willing to spend it to get professional help toward total parish commitment to renewal."

From the first stages of the consultation, misunderstandings began to occur. People held differing impressions about who the consultants were and why they were at St. James. Mac Willson quickly picked up one image of himself. He was surprised at parishioners' reactions when they found out he worked at the spacecraft center.

I was amazed at their awe. It was as though *I* had caused us to put a man on the moon. I found that this was a mixed blessing. They listened attentively to what I had to say but I also had to dispel the notion that I was a provider of panaceas.

Dick Allen feels that he was somewhat responsible for the consultants' strong image because he felt he had to give them a pedigree. Some parishioners saw the consultants as business management people who had know-how on churches. They were "efficiency experts." Others referred to them as "those outside radicals from Houston" or "generals coming in, not saviors." They felt Willson and Persons were saying, "Give us a problem and we'll solve it."

These impressions were perhaps unavoidable because St. James had never used consultants and had never met these two men. Consultants are not people who provide programs or give answers to problems. The idea of con-

sultants as "enablers" of self-change is difficult for a parish to grasp. In fact, St. James actually had to learn to
use consultants. The people of St. James never became
clear about the consultant's role and this lack of clarity
placed severe limits on their change efforts. One active
parishioner put it this way:

I think the issue of the consultation was whether or not we
felt we had a problem. A person doesn't do anything about a
problem unless he knows he's got one. Vasco McCoy (the
senior warden) was able to see our problem. He could see
the deficit and the frustration of Father Allen. Others of us
didn't feel the need. Some even saw Mac and Al as the "hot-
shots from Houston" who were trying to psychoanalyze us.
They felt we did not have that kind of pressing problems.

## VESTRY VOTES ON VAGUE CONTRACT

On May 10, a vestry meeting was held to make a decision about the consultation. The vestry had received an
affirmative recommendation from the group of parishioners who had initially met with Willson. It also received
three very positive letters from parishioners encouraging
the vestry to hire the consultants. At this vestry meeting
several different understandings and opinions about the
consultation began to surface. Vasco McCoy recalls his
concern about the financial problems at St. James:

I had just been elected senior warden and had been told to
go raise money. I saw PTP as a way to raise funds. I pointed
out to the vestry that the consultation was a problem-solving
device and that St. James' first problem was finances. I thought
we should get PTP to help us raise money.

The idea of the consultation solving the parish's financial problems was further reinforced in a letter from one

prestigious parishioner. He wrote that he thought it was a good idea to have parish consultation. He thought that the consultation would probably end up paying for itself if the consultants worked in the parish for several months.

Another vestryman recalls that he voted for the consultation because Vasco was for it and he trusted Vasco. He remembers the senior warden stating that people were moving out of town and leaving the church as they have always done, and that the consultation would help find new people and therefore bring in more money. The consultants would also watch the parish's behavior.

Allen concluded the meeting by sharing his feelings with the vestry:

We need to be unmercifully honest about where we are. If we do have consultation, we might find out that I'm not right for this place. Though we get along well now, we might not later.

After all the discussion, the vestry decided that St. James should enter into consultation with Persons and Willson. Though there was indeed an official decision made by the vestry in favor of parish consultation, in terms of actual commitment the vestry did not decide anything like that. All that can be said is that some of the vestry entered into the consultation. They did not really enter into it for the parish. The vestry said "yes" but not all of them meant "yes." As a total group, the vestry had never met with the consultants. The consultants were not present to explain or negotiate a contract. Willson explained how he saw the vestry functioning.

The vestry doesn't have anything to do with buying and selling. All the vestry has to do is say "yes" or "no." The rector goes into the vestry with a typewritten agenda which he writes up privately. The rector runs the vestry meeting and makes the decisions. The vestry basically is to give credence to his decision.

All of these factors made the consultants' contract very vague. The vestry's lack of understanding and commitment were major hindrances to the effectiveness of Willson and Persons.

The consultants found out about the vestry's decision through the following Sunday's church bulletin. Neither consultant received any direct communication from the rector, the vestry, or the original group. Willson telephoned Dick Allen and asked about the notice and set dates to work on a contract. Allen replied that he had been out of town and had not had time to get in touch with the consultants. Willson reported back to PTP that he saw this incident as indicative of the lack of organization or planning procedures at St. James.

## CONTRACT #1—PARISH PLANNING

Al Persons and Mac Willson went to Texarkana for the weekend of June 1 to gather information and to meet with the vestry. After moving into the rectory living room, they began a three-hour meeting with twelve members representing a cross-section of the parish. The rector, in a letter to these parishioners, had written:

It is expensive to have these highly competent consultants with us, and we must not waste money or time. The value of the project depends upon the participation of certain parish leaders (decision-makers). We have invited only a limited number. The vestry has agreed to enter a contract with the consultant team. PTP is a nationwide project of parish renewal which includes only twelve parishes. You have been selected as one of the twelve. . . . This is not just another unnecessary church meeting.

Al Persons began the meeting by acknowledging his own newness in the parish and finding out that one-third of those present were new to the consultation. Having Al Persons "on stage" first was a carefully planned attempt to have him accepted as a visible member of the consultant team. In order to recapture the flavor of what had gone on at the April visit, several parishioners told of the most significant moments or insights they recalled.

Mac Willson then presented his team's understanding of the purpose of their meeting: "To enable you to set up an organizational overview of the parish and its components in order to identify those areas of the parish where renewal might most fruitfully be implemented." Parishioners checked to see if they were clear about the consultants' purposes and went on to state their expectations of the consultants and of themselves. In his report to PTP, Willson wrote that parishioners said they saw the consultants as resource people who would help the parish assume the responsibility for any changes it needed to make. The parish would move at its own pace, rather than according to some set schedule. This view of the consultants has a different flavor from the overall view of consultants as "fix-it" men.

In order to get an overview of St. James, the parishioners listed areas of concern. They then divided into groups of three to work on questions raised by these concerns. They also looked at the groups which made up the parish and noted the frustrations, conflicts of interest, overlaps, and wholesome relationships they saw. "Underneath all this information is our concern for finances in the face of current needs," noted the senior warden.

Returning to the total group, parishioners organized their findings into identifiable issues:

1. communications

2. involvement
3. management
4. "segregation . . . integration"
5. nebulous socioeconomic picture
6. service to the community

The meeting adjourned after three hours and fifteen minutes. As noted by Al Persons, "The parish tradition is that few show up for any meeting and no meeting runs past two hours." The consultants were beginning to change a parish norm at St. James.

At a luncheon meeting the following day, with 10 of the selected 12 parishioners present, Persons and Willson presented a plan for finding out whether the ideas expressed at last night's meeting were held by most parishioners. They also expressed their desire to help the parish work effectively together on its corporate mission and individual members' financial commitment.

The consultants presented a twofold plan to begin work on the concerns. One direction involved a series of parishwide planning conferences to discover the concerns of the entire parish. A second direction would focus on stewardship education. As reported by Persons, the immediate tone of the meeting was "let's do it." Dates were set for the parish planning conferences and the consultants agreed to write up a summary of the negotiations, which included parish conferences and one vestry meeting to discuss stewardship. The consultants were to mail a contract to the senior warden to sign. The contract was actually signed on June 18, 1970.

Though there were several vestry members among the 12 chosen by the rector to attend these initial meetings, the vestry as a whole never met with the consultants to negotiate this first contract on parish planning. At this meeting with the 12 representatives of the parish, Willson and Persons also briefly shared their ideas on ways to work on finances. They decided to go to the vestry with a separate contract on stewardship education. The consultants were now getting involved in two contracts—a fact that was subsequently to cause problems and confusion.

The consultants also met with the rector, helping him think through his own ability to live with the kind of radical change which involvement in consultation might well engender. They concluded that first visit by realizing that they worked well together. Willson's more confronting stance and Persons's style of supportive encouragement seemed to complement each other.

CONTRACT #2—STEWARDSHIP EDUCATION

The consultant team returned to Texarkana, June 30–July 1, to present a proposal for the stewardship education program to the vestry. They sat in on the first hour and a half of the vestry meeting and observed it. The vestry and rector were trying to make a decision about insulating air-conditioning pipes. Persons and Willson noted that "the rector ran the meeting and set the agenda. The vestrymen asked to be told what to do. More attention was paid to parliamentary procedure than to the problem itself."

The consultants were given the floor after being introduced by the senior warden. Persons and Willson began by presenting a comprehensive plan for stewardship education that had been developed by the Rev. William A. Yon, a consultant from Birmingham, Alabama. Among the criteria included in this complex plan were:

that the pastor was a "tither" or was moving toward it in giving;

that the vestry was also committed to proportionate giving (i.e., tithing);

that the vestry saw the church as spending $1 in the community for each $1 in the parish;

that the vestry was willing to get 25 percent of the congregation to the training meeting;

that the program would be a year-long process.

Vestrymen then raised questions about what the consultants were talking about and how it applied to St. James. They were confused by the differences between the stewardship education plan and the parish planning conferences established in the first contract. When the consultants asked for a vestry commitment, they saw that the vestry members were extremely reluctant to commit themselves individually. It took "tooth-pulling" and individual polling of some of the members to get a commitment. Once it was made, they all seemed to be well satisfied, but as a total group they found it almost impossible to make a decision. The consultants interpreted the difficulties in light of the way the rector and the vestry related to each other:

This time the rector refused to say he was going to do it so we (the consultants) could not get a single soul to commit himself, because the vestry is so programmed to following the leader. They acted as "yes-men" thinking "the rector wants it and he's not going to tell us first but we'll do whatever he says because that's what we always do but we really don't want to."

From the rector's point of view, he was learning and did not want the vestry to "go along" just because he "went along."

At this point in the contract negotiations, expectations and goals became very unclear. Signals were given and missed or mistaken on both sides. The vestry was resistant and the consultants saw their hesitation as indicative of an organizational problem rather than as a "no" answer. The vestry's total commitment to this strenuous educational program was absolutely necessary for its success, and the consultants were unaware of the extent of the vestry's confusion and lack of commitment. Though the vestry members said "yes," they did not fully understand what they were committing themselves to or what that commitment involved. It was not until the consultants were actually in the training sessions that the lack of commitment surfaced. This crucial meeting closed with an invitation to a luncheon meeting the following day on a casual, "come if you can" basis.

The consultants spent the next morning sharing with the rector their data, which indicated that the parish was totally dependent upon him to make all decisions. All parish committees were chaired by the rector. Dick Allen decided he would like to shift much of the administration to competent parishioners. His first step was to ask a lay committee to take care of the publicity and logistics for the up-coming parish planning conferences. The consultants describe Dick Allen's change efforts as follows:

The final coup was the rector's secretary calling to tell the rector that the senior warden was having a meeting the following afternoon. She had been told by the senior warden that the meeting was still on, even though the rector was going to be in Dallas. The rector's verification of that situation apparently came as a total surprise to his secretary.

Allen had never before been able to let people meet without him. Another parish norm was changing to give more responsibility and authority to parishioners. The rector is crucial to change in parish norms. Without his active efforts this change would never have occurred.

Shortly after this meeting, the consultants wrote of Dick Allen:

The rector is aware of the discomfort to be entailed by this change of direction and is still looking forward to the hopes and goals for renewal in spite of his own discomfort. He's a very open, growth-oriented person.

Allen, reflecting on that experience over one year later, recalls:

At the first meeting that Mac and Al attended, there was a big hassle over the pipes. It was torturous. Everybody was waiting for me to decide. Mac and Al really jumped on me. They said, "Here you are, sitting at the head like a papa. Everybody is programmed to you. You raised the questions and you resolved them." I would refuse to sit quietly and let things go unresolved.

Before the consultants left Texarkana on July 1, 1970, they had developed a written proposal for stewardship education. Their overall and original contract consisted of parish planning and a preliminary exploration of stewardship education. Now the stewardship education contract would run concurrently with, or in addition to, the original contract. At this point there were actually two contracts. The consultants' program of stewardship education was complex and dependent on several factors —participation of parishioners, special training for the Every Member Canvass, and evaluation.

## THE FIRST CONTRACT: DISCOVERING ST. JAMES' MISSION AS A PARISH

After the two contracts had been negotiated, the consultants began work on the first contract, helping St.

James work on its mission. Persons and Willson went to Texarkana on July 25 and 26 to conduct two of the three parish planning conferences. *The Messenger* (the parish bulletin) described the conferences:

Answers are not given to us from on high. Answers are "discovered" by members of the parish working together on the mission of the church, using such skills and insights as our consultants will enable us to appropriate. Their purpose is not to tell us what to do, but rather to help us to achieve the goals we ourselves select. And what are our goals? We don't know. This is up to the parish to decide. Your contribution will count. We want everyone to express his or her ideas and this will form the basis for our activities for the future.

All the preconference publicity and logistics were handled by the parishioners under the able leadership of the senior warden. Allen was out of town and contributed nothing to preparations for the conferences. He found his new behavior comfortable enough to continue. The senior warden found that lay people were willing to take on responsibility if it meant heading committees or being in control of specific parts of the work. The physical absence of the rector, along with the self-conscious attempt to let others share responsibility, enabled the senior warden and other parishioners to become more involved in their parish and take on more responsibility.

The first parish planning conference was held on Saturday, July 25, from 9:15 A.M. until 4:00 P.M. The 16 people present addressed the questions: "What do you feel is the best thing that is happening in our life and work at St. James?" and "What would you like to have happen in our life and work at St. James?" After all the answers had been heard, the participants grouped the data into five basic categories of common concerns. The consultants described the general feeling of the participants as: "This is a lot of hard work, but it's worthwhile."

On Sunday an identical planning conference was held after the morning communion service. This time 38 people participated, sharing their ideas about St. James and developing eight categories of common concern. It ended by everyone brainstorming how to involve the rest of the parishioners in the third conference.

On the weekend of August 8 and 9, Mac Willson (Al Persons being on vacation) traveled to Texarkana to conduct the final parish planning conference, which was to be followed by a meeting to pull together the findings of the three conferences. On Saturday morning 23 parishioners participated in the final parish planning conference. The conservative faction of the congregation seemed to be most in evidence and at times used the large plenary sessions to voice its disenchantment with the liberal attitudes of the rector. Willson intervened at several points to keep the participants on their job. The rector found this event difficult because during this same weekend he was weighed down by a painful personal problem that was consuming his energy.

On Sunday, after the morning service, a conference was held to correlate the findings of the three parish planning conferences and develop logistics for starting work on the priority goals. Forty-seven participants and five visitors showed up. All three conferences were represented, although the conference of the previous day was represented in greatest strength. Mac Willson describes the tenor of the meeting as very businesslike. Though still warm toward each other, people were not as playful as before. There was a definite feeling of "today we are going to get something concrete done." The participants reviewed all the areas of common concern and developed five interest areas on which to work. They divided into five groups to consider:

1. Youth and the church
2. Administration
3. Worship and liturgy
4. Mission within the parish
5. Mission outside the parish.

Each group established priorities about what it wanted to do before the consultants returned on September 26. Each took steps to organize and to implement the ideas. Looking back on the culmination of that work, Willson expressed his feeling that it was an unqualified success and that St. James had a lot of momentum at that point.

INITIAL WORK ON STEWARDSHIP EDUCATION

The parish and the consultants began work in the early fall on the vestry's contract for stewardship education. Traditionally the senior warden had always served as chairman of the Every Member Canvass. This year, after consulting with Father Allen, some influential parishioners, and the two consultants, he decided to make a conscious attempt to shift parish leadership from the ingrained leaders to new parishioners. Recognizing the risk involved in such a radical change, McCoy appointed two newcomers to head up the canvass. Though these two people brought freshness and new energy to the task, as leaders they had little influence because they were newcomers. Over the next months McCoy and the others who were trying to change patterns were to learn from hard experience that St. James was not ready for this kind of shift in leadership.

On Friday evening the consultants held the first meeting with a nine-person steering committee appointed by the vestry. They were for the most part wives of influential men in the town and parish. Since the education of people in terms of stewardship is quite different from the traditional method of signing a pledge card, the consultants went over in detail the criteria, the training, and the general design for the stewardship education program. They explained that the success of the program was based on parish commitment. If the parish leaders were not highly motivated or willing to give of themselves, then the effect would be minimal. The committee members raised questions and concerns which showed a high level of anxiety that seemed to increase. In light of their task, the group's anxiety proved realistic. After clarifying the design and steps to be taken, the group reviewed its function and responsibility as a steering committee and set up dates for training. The meeting ended in a spirit of "let's get it done."

FOLLOW-UP ON PARISH PLANNING

On Saturday morning of that same weekend, the consultants shifted directions and again worked on their initial contract concerning parish planning. They met on Saturday morning with representatives of the five task forces established in August. The consultants expected 50 people but only 14 showed up. Each group reported on what it had done and discussed the problems it was having. Several groups appeared confused over their goals and seemed to lack direction; only one had begun any work. The parish administration group reported on a parish survey to be done in late October which would include the gathering of demographic data and the identification of parishioners' skills and talents. Several other committee representatives also expressed their need for a parish survey. In closing, the group decided to meet again approximately two weeks after the information from the parish survey had been assembled.

Willson and Persons later commented on the discouraging reports of the task forces:

The various task forces have few if any skills in administration or manpower development, so they are up against a gap between excitement and willingness on the one hand and a lack of know-how on the other. Four of the five task forces are having rough sledding and experiencing deep frustration. Therefore, we are putting together a report to the parish, recommending the necessary training and options. We think that we have held out a high hope to the parish through goal-setting operations and have not offered sufficient change theory or practice for them to bear the responsibility called for. In short, we have a new hope intellectually and old attitudes at the gut level. How we handle this discrepancy is crucial to our entire relationship with St. James.

In this instance either people did not know or they misunderstood what was expected of them; therefore, they did not understand or initiate any continuing efforts.

## BACK TO STEWARDSHIP: PARISH NORMS
## AFFECT TRAINING

Several weeks later, Persons and Willson again went to Texarkana to concentrate on the stewardship education program. On the weekend of October 16–18, the consultants conducted two six-hour training sessions on stewardship. Some 30 people had promised to attend, but only six people showed up for the first half of the training and three more showed up for the second half. The consultants thought the lack of response was caused by (1) lack of organization within the parish—partially a failure of the vestry to communicate what they had committed themselves to in the first place; and (2) the consultants' efforts to move into an area for which the members did not have the necessary basic skills.

Prior to the six-hour training sessions, co-chairman Mrs. Wanda Burns telephoned parishioners asking them to come. Several responded to her request with, "Oh, no, not another long weekend!" They felt pressured, and they resented having to spend so much time for another parish event. Several explained that the September season was a busy time for families because of community activities and football games. Discovering this resistance, Mrs. Burns telephoned Willson and Persons in Houston. She expressed her doubts about the number of people who would come and asked the consultants to shorten the training session. She felt that Willson and Persons were unwilling to change the schedule; they were using this stewardship program for the first time and did not feel that they could modify the original plans.

Several parishioners who did attend those training sessions have clear ideas about the attendance problem. One put it this way:

Mac and Al had fixed ideas about the six-hour sessions. People simply weren't going to give that much time. People were beginning to open up, but not enough for a weekend.

Another parishioner remembers his discomfort:

I'd cringe over the sparse attendance. People were scared off by the time (factor). I was ashamed of the parish and embarrassed for Mac and Al. The vestry was not dedicated. They were apathetic. Texarkana and the parish are both apathetic. They both need shaking and a shot in the arm.

Concerned about the lack of attendance at the training session, Mac Willson telephoned the rector and the senior warden in November, asking them to bring up with the vestry his feelings that the parish had not lived up to its commitment to the stewardship education contract. It was as though the vestry had said "yes" to the contract but really meant "no" to having 25 percent of the parish receive the training and participate in the program. For the stewardship education program to be successful, it was essential that vestry members and parish leaders not only actively participate and support the program, but also accept training for this new style of stewardship education which was very different from the traditional Every Member Canvass.

Also, in November, the leaders of the stewardship program made their first personal contact with the rest of the parish. Canvassers had held evening meetings in several parishioners' homes, and the rector gave the hosts and hostesses lists of parishioners to invite. The consultants noted that there was status in being invited to certain influential parishioners' homes. The meetings were either a roaring success or a complete failure, depending on who was invited to what home. For example, one of the newer members of St. James had a gathering at her home and invited 70 people. Twenty of them promised to come and only two showed up. This phenomenon was totally unexpected.

Some parishioners who had spent a great deal of time and energy were upset and hurt by the lack of response. These home meetings proved to be divisive to parish life. The consultants learned from this situation the power of social norms at St. James. Since parish norms are corporate ways of behavior that develop slowly over a long period of time, a parish is often unaware of them. Unfortunately for St. James' stewardship efforts, the norm that people will not attend meetings at homes of persons without influence had to be learned by the consultants from experience.

After reviewing events, Willson described his feelings:

"This has to have been the low point in our consultation. I am now looking forward to a bigger and better 1971."

At this point several interrelated ideas and ways of operating at St. James surfaced. St. James has parishioners with different needs. Some want more social fellowship. Others see the church as solely a "religious" place. Newcomers do not feel very welcome. People will only attend meetings at homes of influential parishioners. People resist coming to long meetings during times of family and community activity. All of these factors say something about life at St. James, or at least they point to how things are done. The way a parish acts is indicative of who it is. It is unusual to find a parish that is willing to pay such close attention to its way of "doing things" and then ask what these norms say about the parish's identity. At St James, consultants were able to help the parish begin to identify the norms, see their effect, and then attempt to change unproductive patterns to more fulfilling ways of behavior. St. James and the consultants have learned that this is a difficult experience.

REVIEWING THE CONSULTATION

The year of 1971 began with an informal review of the consultation. Several months had passed since the consultants' last visit, so they wanted to catch up on how things were going. On January 11, the two consultants met with Dick Allen and the senior warden and his wife at the Willsons' home in Houston. Both Dick Allen and the McCoys praised the consultants for the job they had done and hoped for a continuing relationship. They also provided the consultants with a different perspective on the stewardship education program. The three of them felt that the stewardship program had been successful.

The McCoys and Dick Allen went on to state their

opinions that the consultants had made too many assumptions about the sophistication of parishioners when it came to financial matters. They explained that many parishioners were not willing to discuss money in a social setting, and they were also unwilling to spend six hours in a church meeting. One evening meeting would have been more acceptable. The senior warden, though greatly concerned about the financial plight of St. James, regretted that the consultation had shifted from parish planning to raising money. People were confused about the consultants' overall purpose.

Allen and the McCoys also reported that the parish survey, which was supposed to be done in October, had not been begun. They very much wanted to administer the survey in order to get more definitive information about who made up St. James and what resources were in the parish. As one of them put it, "We still don't know where 75 percent of the parish is. So far we have touched only 25 percent." In conclusion, the group reported that only one of the five committees created by the planning conference was active. Before leaving, Allen, the McCoys, and the consultants discussed the possibility of a future relationship between St. James and the consultants. All agreed that the two parties needed to renegotiate their financial agreement.

On January 25, St. James held its annual parish meeting. Willson and Persons wrote a detailed review of the consultation for this meeting. The report took the form of seven reflections. In summary, they were:

1. The consultants greatly appreciated the parish's willingness to undertake serious and extensive efforts toward renewal.
2. A representative cross section of the parish had been involved in the consultation and significant learnings

had been made for PTP and for St. James.

3. The consultants found some people willing to give more time than they had anticipated, and at the same time they found some people not yet willing to give the time that such work involved.

4. Parishioners had grown more aware of how decisions were made and work carried out. They had grown increasingly responsible for St. James' life.

5. There was an increasing number of parishioners beginning to experience the freedom to say "no" instead of saying "yes" and meaning "no."

6. There seemed to be a new initiative for accepting and and carrying out tasks.

7. Parish commitment was hampered by (a) assumptions on the part of many people that to try something different is to risk failure, which will not be forgiven and must, therefore, be avoided, (b) an absence of any ongoing training.

Willson and Persons made three suggestions for future work:

1. That they sit in with groups to gain a broader and deeper picture of the organizational life of St. James.

2. That they continue to work on the goals already developed.

3. That they begin specialized training to sharpen effectiveness within the parish.

At that same parish meeting St. James faced a severe financial problem, with an $8,000 deficit for 1970. There was no money at that time to pay the consultants; in fact, the parish was having to decide whether or not to let the curate go because of lack of funds. The team had no written contract after its closure date of April 1, 1971.

There was, however, a gentlemen's agreement that both sides wished to continue the consultation.

While McCoy and Allen, the two men most involved and fully understanding the consultation, wanted very much to continue it, the newly elected vestry began to lose interest and commitment. In February, shortly after the annual parish meeting, Mac Willson telephoned Vasco McCoy to discuss the possibility of a vestry weekend conference for team-building and work effectiveness. McCoy, believing in the value of a vestry conference, went to the vestry with the consultants' proposal. He reported that the vestry's negative reaction made him feel as though he were really left all alone. The vestrymen did not want a conference and they felt that PTP was trying to control them. "By February," said Vasco McCoy, "we had been through the wringer. We were tired. I was the only vestryman still flying the flag for the consultation. At least this time we were not afraid to say 'no' to the idea of a vestry weekend."

CLARIFYING THE CONSULTANTS' RELATIONSHIP

Al Persons and Mac Willson, desiring to learn as much as possible from their experience, returned to Texarkana on the weekend of May 15 and 16 to get an honest evaluation of where St. James was at that point as compared to where it had been prior to the consultation. They had hoped to get an accurate reading on reactions to the consultation and also wanted to clarify their future relationship. PTP's national office in Washington paid for the visit since funds were so limited at St. James.

Father Allen reported that the vestry's finance committee was working on its own and doing very well with little or no help from the rector. Committee members were actively alerting parishioners to the current financial crisis.

Since the chairman was a vestryman, this marked a shift in leadership from the rector and the senior warden toward a vestry member. Allen went on to speak of his own personal growth:

I can let go of a lot of things that I used to do compulsively. I think the fact that I can go home at 9:00 and watch TV with my family and not feel I have to be at the office represents growth on my part. I can even sit and do nothing at times. Yet I occasionally feel guilty, too. I can refer others to tasks rather than always do them myself. I'm not as uptight as I used to be and I feel less need to justify myself. I'm less involved in the numbers game now.

Vasco McCoy informed Willson and Persons that the Lenten meetings in parishioners' homes were now emphasizing both Holy Communion and fellowship. This new tack was a result of the learnings about social norms from the stewardship experience. In terms of the specific learnings about stewardship education, McCoy reported that most of the parish never understood what the consultation was all about. The two contracts were confused and many attended the stewardship education program with no idea of what was going on. Others understood the purpose of the parish planning conference, but not Project Test Pattern as an experimental project. Allen emphasized the fact that the purpose of the parish planning conferences was to give the parish a chance to change its life style, but those attending did not know what the life style was at that time.

In order to get a broader picture of St. James, on Sunday morning the consultants led both the 7:45 congregation and the 10:00 congregation through the long-overdue parish survey. A total of 156 questionnaires were filled out. Directly after the Sunday morning service Willson and Persons met with the vestry to review the consultation's history, to develop and share learnings, and then to talk about a future relationship. The vestry decided to hold a meeting with the entire congregation on June 13 to vote on whether or not to continue the consultation. But June 13 brought a new emergency to St. James. The parish and vestry had to discuss its air-conditioning problem and the decision on consultation was postponed until July. In the meantime, the consultants reported to the vestry on the results of the parish survey. They recommended specific ways to move, based on the gathered information. One vestryman explained that although the vestry did receive the consultants' report, he felt that the steam had gone out of things by that time. No one ever studied the report.

TERMINATION

On the weekend of July 11, Mac Willson and his family rearranged their vacation itinerary in order to have one more significant amount of time with Dick Allen, Vasco McCoy, and the vestry. Their primary topic of discussion at Saturday's meeting with the rector and senior warden was St. James' financial straits. On Sunday Willson met with the vestry and carefully explained the conditions for continuing the consultation. He noted that the vestry expressed no problem with his conditions except for the financial arrangements. They had no money for any additional or outside items for the 1971 fiscal year. The vestry tabled any further action until they got the new financial figures for the next year. Although St. James' financial crisis and the vestry's indecisive actions suggest a desire to terminate the relationship, the vestry nevertheless stated that they did not want to terminate the relationship. Willson closed by inviting St. James to telephone the consultants if they felt the need. The consultants and

the vestry agreed that if St. James could afford to continue, the two parties would renegotiate a contract when
funds were available.

Reflecting on that final arrangement in their report to
PTP, Willson and Persons both noted that they had no
feelings of needing to hang on to St. James. In fact, they
felt that in many ways it would be easier to start afresh
with a new parish, applying some of the learnings from
the past contract. At the same time Vasco McCoy wanted
very much for Mac and Al to continue at St. James to
help the parish reap the benefits of the ground work that
had been done.


ISSUES AND LEARNINGS

1  POWER OF PARISH NORMS

Over the years St. James has developed ways of doing
things which are taken for granted or assumed. St. James,
like most parishes and most people, was unaware of the
patterns it had grown into and how these ways influenced
and molded its life. St. James' story indicates the strength
of norms on parish life.

a) *Parish norms are related to community norms.* Both
Texarkana and St. James share an ambivalence toward
change. The city values its traditional and relaxed style
of life and at the same time wants to change and find
new ways of living (*e.g.*, the Model Cities Programs).
St. James also balances these two forces of tradition and
change. It opens its doors to blacks, yet has difficulty
accepting newcomers. Some parishioners feel Texarkana
has closed social groups that carry over to church life.
Parishioners only attend meetings at homes of influential members. Prestige is attached to being invited
to these homes. Some newcomers do not feel welcome

and some long-time parishioners also desire a closer sense of community and fellowship.

b) *Parish norms affect the work of the consultants.* At the beginning of the consultation, one of St. James' norms was that the rector made all the decisions and the vestry acted as "yes men" to the rector. Consequently, the vestry accepted a vague contract for consultation. Only the rector and the senior warden felt the need and were committed to consultation. The vestry, not seeing the problem, never really committed itself and never assumed responsibility. Nor did parishioners assume responsibility for tasks after the parish planning conferences or during stewardship education. Agreeing to do something at St. James did not mean much. The consultants had difficulty enabling the parish to implement goals because committees did not meet and people did not show up for training sessions. St. James' parish norms inhibited lay people from assuming and carrying through on responsibility. Lay people felt little ownership for the parish or the consultation.

c) *Parish norms are extremely difficult to change.* Patterns of behavior that have developed slowly over a long period of time become deeply entrenched. The way a parish lives its life is indicative of its nature. When parish norms change, the actual self-image and identity of the parish change. Producing these changes is extremely hard work. Not only did St. James have to identify the norms that were operating, but it then had to risk failure and make a self-conscious attempt to shift. A change in norms is a radical change. Often when something is done that violates a norm, it tends to be negated. Vasco McCoy intentionally violated a norm at St. James by having newcomers run the Every Member Canvass. Allen intentionally violated a norm by not giving the vestry answers and by allowing parishioners to organize the parish planning conferences.

Recognizing a need does not necessarily mean commitment to do anything about it. People are able to see the need to change, they are able to identify the effects, yet they are often unable to change even when they want to. St. James' task forces wanted to work on goals, yet they did not follow through with their work. The vestry heard the financial problems, agreed to a program of stewardship education and then did not carry out the efforts needed. St. James had a norm of saying "yes" but not following through. People found it difficult to say "no." Changing parish norms is perhaps the most difficult task for a consultant and a parish. It takes a great deal of strength to sustain the long-term, self-conscious efforts which change and permanent growth require. For St. James and its consultants even to attempt to change norms was a brave undertaking.

## 2  IMPORTANCE OF A CLEAR CONTRACT

A consultant once commented that if he ever satisfactorily negotiated a clear contract, he really did not have to do any more. Negotiating a contract involves teaching a parish how to use consultants. St. James had never used consultants and had to learn how. Persons and Willson learned the absolute necessity of clear communications and understandings. Consultants need constantly to clarify where their clients are. They can never take for granted that people understand what is going on. Vague negotiations between the consultants and St. James severely limited the possibilities for change. Parishioners held exaggerated images of the consultants and their role in the parish. Vestry members did not understand the purpose of the consultation, nor did they support the change efforts. They were ambivalent about their need for consultation and were confused about their goals. When the consultants introduced a second contract, the vestry was doubly confused. Members did not understand the difference between the stewardship education program and a traditional Every Member Canvass. The confusion between stewardship education and parish planning efforts resulted in minimal commitment from St. James. St. James did not have the internal strength to sustain intense work on two contracts simultaneously. It diffused the client's energy, efforts, and morale, and they became discouraged.

### 3 CONSULTANTS' PERSONALITY INFLUENCES THE PARISH

Besides having special skills in organization development and group process, the team also brings to the parish its own unique assets and personality. Willson and Persons brought several ingredients to St. James that seem to stand out. They paid close attention to how they worked together as a team. During his first visit with St. James, Al Persons was up front and on stage. This was a planned and deliberate attempt to bring him on board, since St. James had previously only seen Willson. The two men also seemed to complement each other in styles of operating. Persons provided the more supportive aspect, while Willson provided the more confrontive stance. Both had a strong desire to learn all they could from their experience. They were constantly working on learnings in order to be more effective and helpful. One member of the team, Al Persons, was a long-time personal friend of Dick Allen. From the slight data on their friendship, one might gather that a previous friendship brought a degree of immediate trust between the consultants and the rector.

4  RECTOR'S OPENNESS IS CRUCIAL TO PARISH'S CHANGE EFFORTS

Without the full cooperation and active support of the rector, a parish experiences little, if any, changes. Dick Allen felt a need for change, was open to taking an honest look at himself, and was able to try new alternatives. Being supported and confronted by the consultants, Allen made a conscious attempt to change his style of leadership. He began to let others take on responsibility and make decisions. This change in behavior took great effort. Allen was supported in his change efforts by the senior warden, Vasco McCoy. McCoy and Allen developed a remarkable team working to shift the patterns of behavior and ways of doing things at St. James.

a) *Ownership and Initiative Shifts from Rector to Vestry to Parish Groups.* Dick Allen willingly let others assume new and greater responsibility. In turn, the vestry began to feel a greater sense of ownership for St. James. It became more the lay people's church and not just the rector's. As this shift began to occur, the atmosphere in the vestry became smoother, freer, and more relaxed. Allen personally felt freer, more relaxed, less pressured. With Allen and the vestry sharing responsibility, Allen felt less need to do it all himself. The vestry began to feel free to say no and express negativity. The vestry began to hold committee meetings without the rector and even gave important parish responsibility to people not on the vestry. A vestry committee on finance did a productive job without the help of the rector or the senior warden.

Allen noted that since the consultation he had found more people willing to give of their time. Fourteen teachers of the Bethel Bible Series, for example, meet with the rector for two and a half hours per week, and then study for eight to twelve hours per week without him. The women's group and the acolytes are also moving along at their own pace, without the rector. A couple's club, the Saints and Sinners, was started in January, 1971, and has continued to meet for dinner and fellowship once a month. This group, which was organized and operates without the rector, has grown rapidly and has helped to meet the social needs of newcomers and other parishioners.

## 5 CONSULTATION CHANGES ATMOSPHERE AT ST. JAMES

In speaking about the consultation, parishioners claim they have become more sensitive and aware of the work of the rector. Some see his job as discouraging, others seem to appreciate the hard work that goes into being rector of St. James. Parishioners went on to note a change in atmosphere. St. James seemed to develop a warmer and stronger sense of fellowship and community. At the parish planning conferences, people grew to trust each other and to know each other better. They began to express criticism for the first time and now felt that their opinions were important and valuable. Though apathy still remains a problem, St. James now has more active, contributing members. It is not possible to know exactly how many people were affected by the consultation. The consultants felt that if they had been able to make contact with more people earlier in their efforts, changes would have been deeper and broader.

## CONCLUSION

The case of St. James gives several clear learnings about parishes and change. Parish and social norms are powerful, and hard work is necessary to change these patterns of behavior. Its story also points out specialized learnings for consultants in the area of communications and contract negotiations. The overall impression of St. James' story is as important as the specific learnings. For St. James' Church planned and purposeful change was a difficult and demanding process. The very attempt toward change took a lot of courage and risk. Its story emphasizes the complexity and the time needed to plan change and growth.

# 6

## THE STORY OF THE CHURCH OF THE
## TRANSFIGURATION

Birmingham, the largest city in Alabama, with a population reaching toward three quarters of a million, is a city struggling with an identity change. It has been a steel town; it is also becoming a medical and educational center. There are fourteen Episcopal churches in the city, each with its own style of life and brand of churchmanship, but most of them serving the affluent "over-the-mountain" area south of the city.

In the spring of 1970, the youngest of these congregations, the Church of the Transfiguration, was worrying about its future. Its vicar, the Rev. Bob Ross, had been enthusiastic about starting an experimental church as free as possible from tradition, and based on some of the values and procedures of the Group Life Lab. In an article in *The Episcopalian* (May 1970) he wrote about the beginnings of that congregation in Birmingham, Alabama:

What we set out to do was to develop a congregation which would:

—Make some kind of clear commitment a condition for membership.

—Move rapidly toward financial independence by having no investment in real estate or furnishings.

—Develop forms of worship appropriate to the informal gathering places it would use.

—Seek out those supposedly disinterested, especially teen-agers, young married couples, and professional people, in the hope that new approaches would appeal to them.

—Provide a platform for local ecumenicity. In other words, have an Episcopal parish without being denominational.

—Develop a kind of congregational life in which leadership and ministry are truly shared.

—Seek ways of getting with a transient society and being the church for people on the move.

Twenty-five or thirty people, many of them from neighboring parishes, had been committing themselves to meeting on Sundays at the "Y" or in people's yards for a flexible, informal liturgy and for small groups, which "self-destructed" and re-formed every thirteen weeks. Like parishioners of other Birmingham Episcopal churches, most members of this two-year-old mission came from "over the mountain." They were, however, a younger and less conventional group of people than those served by other churches, with an average age of twenty-eight and socially liberal, activist attitudes. Eight or ten of the group were doctors, there were two priests and two lawyers, and several others in the helping professions. They wanted an intimate, relaxed kind of community which spoke meaningfully to their lives and the life they saw around them. In the summertime, they like to come bare-footed, wearing comfortable, casual clothes, to the backyard celebrations. Bob Ross describes his parishioners as "an attractive, turned-on group of people, with sparkling personalities." In the spring of '70, interpersonal intensity, commitment, and pledges were high. The board of trustees was a rotational body rather than an elected one,

and the vicar saw the leadership of the congregation as a responsibility shared by all members. "I began to wonder," wrote Bob Ross in *The Episcopalian*, "if a congregation like this needed a priest at all."

There were ambivalent reactions to the intense T-group kind of involvement. Some members made comments like these:

"The intimacy is great but I can't take it all the time."

"It was difficult to decide on anything. We had to stop and deal with feelings all the time."

"It's divided my family—my daughter and husband didn't go, and I did."

"It's a place for people on the way out and on the way in. I would like to see them reach out to others."

Looking back, Loren Mead, director of Project Test Pattern, wrote:

Spring of 1970—there was a sense of "waiting" in the congregation, a sort of wondering what was coming next. The minister and a number of members of the congregation were increasingly anxious about "growth"—why it hadn't happened, what it would mean if it did happen, what would happen to the congregation if it didn't "make it" financially.

## ARK OR LIFEBOAT?

During the same spring the Rev. Charles L. Winters, Jr., professor of systematic theology at the Seminary of the South, Sewanee, Tenn. and the Rev. Herbert A. Donovan, Jr., at that time assistant to the bishop of the Diocese of Kentucky, were looking for a suitable client parish with which to consult. They were under contract to Project Test Pattern to seek and negotiate a contract with a client, report regularly to PTP, accept consultation as suggested and as feasible, and negotiate for adequate payment for their services. Expenses not covered in the contract would be reimbursed by PTP.

Winters and Donovan looked at two parishes—one six years old and fairly settled, the other the Church of the Transfiguration, where, Herb Donovan felt, the people were afraid the bishop would say, "If you don't get self-supporting by such and such a date, I'm closing you up."

Months later, the vicar of Transfiguration readily admitted that he had experienced some anxiety about getting involved in the consultation. He recalled that he only took action when he heard that Winters was to be on the team. He had had a close relationship with Winters at seminary and had a lot of trust in him.

On May 6, Winters and Donovan wrote to Loren Mead that they had made a decision to enter contract negotiations with Transfiguration. They felt that the lab orientation of the group would provide a foundation for organization development work, and they were intrigued by this unusual mission and the learnings they felt might come from working with it.

At the exploratory meeting in March, Bob Ross had called together all interested parishioners to talk with Donovan and Winters about the possibility of a consultation. The two consultants described PTP and told the group what was involved in a consultative relationship. The Transfiguration people talked about their joys and their problems, which the consultants summarized in their report: "Two major concerns expressed were the problem of growth, or the lack of it, and the problem of becoming financially self-supporting, a burden that the group felt was being imposed on them by the bishop."

As they talked over their reactions to this meeting, Winters and Donovan had four subjective impressions of their prospective client as a result of the visit of this group:

1. There was a deep involvement and commitment to the mission and to one another.
2. There was a real "wondering about" what it means and how to express it; that is, one's involvement and commitment.
3. There was obviously a willingness to T-group at the drop of a hat.
4. Regarding the issue of decision-making by consensus, there was a tremendous desire in this group to develop a trust relationship which can only come this way. There seemed to be a euphoric idea that this was "arrival."

Charles Winters had previously accepted an invitation to the mission to preach at a Good Friday service two days after the meeting. He was impressed, during the informal, spontaneous service, by the number of people with deep individual needs and problems for whom belonging to this community was very important. After the service, he had a chance to talk alone with Bob Ross, who "described his own sense of frustration and alienation from his fellow clergy in the institutional church, the feeling that he was on an ark rather than a lifeboat with a line back to the mother church."

Bob Ross, an intelligent and articulate clergyman, liked to wrestle with some of the problems about his ministry and his mission by writing articles and papers. During the spring of 1970 he wrote a paper called "The Modular Parish," in which he repeated his observation that "the franchised and replicated popular institutional structure which we have inherited, enshrined in plastic, and then set up in the suburbs has a very limited appeal and effectiveness." Ross had been impressed by a lecture given by Dr. John Fletcher, Director of Inter-Met, at an Alabama clergy conference. Fletcher spoke about how the values of an industrial society (such as quantity, delay of gratification, achievement-orientation, and emotional neutrality) are giving way to new values appropriate to the post-industrial era in which we live, values concerned with quality of life, individuality, an adaptive approach to living, and involvement. Ross saw these values as marks of Transfiguration's life style. He was beginning to think that perhaps the mission was able to embody these values precisely because it was small, and that maybe "we expected to grow up to be a peach tree when what we are is a strawberry plant!" He suggested that the pressures driving churches toward larger membership might be better met by creating federations of small worshipping entities. In spite of this insight, the congregation found itself concerned about growth in numbers and financial strength.

SIGNING A CONTRACT

On May 27, Winters and Donovan met with Ross and nine members of the mission (some had come to the earlier meeting, others had not) to negotiate a contract. The consultants summarized the concerns they had heard expressed at the March meeting—about growth, finances, the relationship with the bishop and the rest of the diocese, and "what the congregation was in business for—one another, or something else."

In the discussion that followed, several other concerns that the group thought should be issues in the consultation were brought up.

1. What is our relationship to tradition? Are we really as free as we think we are?
2. How can we deal with differences as they come up, instead of saving them for community meetings?
3. Why have some people become isolated from the group?
4. There was agreement that the mission needed to work on its relationship with neighboring Episcopal churches.
5. What is the relationship of the congregation to Bob Ross, and of the mission to the Church at large?
6. Bob and Flower Ross expressed concern about maintenance-man jobs using up time which should be spent "getting out" or "just being."

This summary of the issues for consultation was accepted by the group. After considerable discussion of financial arrangements, Winters and Donovan offered to put in writing a proposal for a contract, leaving a blank space for Transfiguration to fill in a proposed fee. The consultants suggested that they would begin their work by collecting data and would then propose issues they felt they could help the mission work on.

A lot of uncertainty about who was really the client was expressed much later in the consultation. There were those who felt PTP was the client: "We were doing this for the national Church." Many felt the vicar was the client, and that others were denied direct access to the consultants. There were differences of opinion about whether the changing ad hoc group present at contract negotiations really represented the congregation.

In any event, on July 6 Loren Mead received word that the contract had been signed. The congregation had set the consultants' fee as six percent of gross receipts plus a special offering from the members. The consultants accepted this proposal as evidence of substantial commitment, even though it did not cover expenses and the consultants' travel costs had to be subsidized by PTP. At the Birmingham Retrieval Conference the following November, Herb Donovan talked about the mission's unusual method of paying the consultants: "For that special offering, incidentally, they made themselves a little box with flowers on it. I asked them to make 'Herb Boxes' and 'Charlie Boxes' and then at the end we could see who got the most, to see who was the most effective consultant, but Charlie was too chicken." This sally was greeted with hoots of laughter. "Very creative of you!" was the comment of a fellow consultant.

PRESENTING THE DATA

From June 25 to 27, Winters and Donovan visited Birmingham to conduct data-gathering interviews with members and former members of the mission, several neighboring clergy, and diocesan staff members. Transfiguration members were interviewed by one consultant, clergy often by both. At the Birmingham Retrieval Conference these comments were made:

Donovan: There was a real desire on their part to know how they were perceived outside the congregation, particularly by the neighboring clergy.
Mead: This congregation has a real anxiety about its environment?
Donovan: Right.

At the end of the June visit, the consultants observed Transfiguration's quarterly "regrouping" meeting. Members were asked to suggest, and sign up for, the kinds of groups they would be interested in working in for the next thirteen weeks. The consultants' impression of this gathering was that it was a "confused, disorganized group where the people who spoke the most and the loudest were in control, and where there were a good number of people who seemed bored with the whole procedure."

Because of last-minute schedule difficulties, Donovan was unable to be present at the second series of data-gathering interviews on July 25 to 27. Charles Winters talked with members, two more clergy, and two groups of children.

The consultants spent twenty-four hours together organizing the data gathered during their June and July visits to Birmingham and preparing two separate reports. The report on data about the mission would be presented to the congregation; the report about the vicar was to be made available to Bob Ross, who would have the option of keeping it as a confidential report or sharing it with mission members—which, as it developed, he was eager to do.

On August 31 both reports were presented in writing to the entire group. They studied the answers members and neighboring clergy had given to the consultants' questions: how they saw the strengths and weaknesses of the mission and its relationship with other congregations; and how they would describe the vicar's ministry. The group was then asked, "As you look at the data, what simile comes to mind? Transfiguration is like what?" Some of the responses were: "a great collection of almosts," "to clergy a wart on the body of Christ," "a little child in the wilderness, sacred, hollering for help," "people holding hands facing inward."

Along with positive responses to Bob Ross's warmth and leadership abilities, the report on the vicar contained indications that the very strength of that leadership was provoking reactions. One comment was that "Bob's large stake obliged things to go his way." Reactions from neighboring clergy were generally negative. They felt that the vicar came on too strong and they resented what they saw as an isolated, free-wheeling, perhaps even irresponsible, operation. The report on the vicar could apparently not be dealt with by the group until some time later. Loren Mead reported a year from the following September: "That night and for some time afterward there was considerable questioning of that information [about the vicar and the mission]. Some characterized the questioning as 'fighting the data,' while others saw it as questioning the data base."

A third section of the consultants' report, presented the evening of August 31, listed the issues they saw emerging from the data:

I. Internal issues
   A. Decision-making—How well is consensus working, as a way of making decisions? What is the rector's role in the decision-making process?
   B. Acceptance—Who is included? Excluded?
   C. Children—What is their place in the mission? What do they need?
II. External issues
   A. Finances—Transfiguration's resentment of financial pressures from outside; outsiders' resentment of Transfiguration's dependent status, freedom from property, and full-time vicar.
   B. Outreach—Criticisms about the mission's being "ingrown and inward looking."
   C. Relationship to the rest of the Church—Can there be mutual offerings?

Donovan and Winters spent the morning and afternoon of September 1 preparing to present their own reactions to the data. They developed a theory that they decided to offer to the group that evening. They described Transfiguration as a community caught between two conflicting models:

1. Transfiguration had consciously modeled itself on the Group Life Lab, whose primary characteristics are:
    a. High motivation and intense commitment.
    b. A short-term involvement.
    c. Limited membership and, once underway, inability to admit new members.
2. Transfiguration was also a congregation of the Protestant Episcopal Church, and as such was called upon to embrace these characteristics:
    a. Varying levels of commitment.
    b. Long-term membership.
    c. The inclusion of as many members as possible.

The laboratory model constituted the essence of the mission's uniqueness and could not be abandoned; but it had led to an ingrown image and to difficulty in accepting new people. How can a lab recruit? On the other hand, how can a congregation achieve the kind of commitment and growth that were important marks of Transfiguration's life? "The consultants," according to their report, "then made a suggestion for dealing with the apparent contradiction between the models: regard the present group as providing a nucleus from which might come leadership for establishing other groups. That is, instead of trying to assimilate new members into a group whose history made it difficult to enter, allow new groups to form and develop their own history, with the aid of trained members of the nuclear group. By their own testimony, the members' children felt themselves to be related to the mission but not really a part of it. Therefore, this group was suggested as a possible opportunity to test this plan of action."

Donovan and Winters hoped, by this analysis, to free the group from the power of the contradiction in which the mission had been caught but which it had not understood. The congregation began to look for the values of the laboratory model within the short-term, self-destructing groups, rather than in the mission as a total entity. Some members expressed less positive reactions to the theory input in September 1971: "That laboratory vs. congregation method—I don't think I like it." "It started the second biggest fight we ever had." "We don't have a good handle on it." "I thought it was accurate though painful."

The consultants later questioned the wisdom of their suggestion, partly because problem-solving was not their function, and partly because their attempts in that direction fell on deaf ears. But it would have been almost impossible to resist offering an idea which was so clearly relevant to the inner conflicts of the mission, the modular theories of the vicar, and the dissatisfaction with what the mission had been able to offer its children.

The board of trustees and the mission as a whole continued to wrestle with the consultants' report after Donovan and Winters had left Birmingham. On September 30, the board of trustees wrote the consultants a letter. "Many people," they wrote, "had difficulty in seeing the relationship between the data you gathered and the proposals for action you made. Many other people felt content with the data and proposals. . . ." The board wanted to continue with the consultation, but wanted to know who the consultants considered their client to be—the whole congregation? the board? the vicar? others? They expressed frustration about the geographical and schedule difficulties that made it impossible for the consultants to visit again for two months. "There are four areas," they went on, "where we feel a need for help, and where we have groups of people organizing for action and *asking* for consultative help." They designated these four areas as: worship, children, money, and new people.

The board of trustees' letter had pinpointed two of the problems in the consultation at this point: the lack of clarity as to who the client was, and the inability of the consultants to schedule more regular and frequent trips to Birmingham. Winters and Donovan had also been feeling a more internal kind of problem, an uncertainty whether they, as fairly traditional churchmen, could be wholly sympathetic with this way-out mission. They reported that, at dinner, "the vicar expressed a real concern that the consultants might be trying to *reform* him and that they did not like *his baby* (the mission). He seemed to be reassured by the conversation that resulted." But the consultants felt it was important to be fully aware of their own presuppositions, and thought it likely that this issue would come up again.


DEFINING THE VICAR'S JOB

During the months that followed, the task forces concerned with the four major problem areas went to work, with uneven success. A small group met briefly on the money issue, and then became inactive. The "inclusion" group found that it had two separate problems to deal with, and it split into two subgroups to consider: (a) the problem of the mission member who needed to be included; and (b) the problem of including newcomers and strangers. The "inside inclusion" group did not continue to function. The "outside inclusion" group wrote a brochure explaining the mission. One member said, "It started as a group and turned into a committee!"

By the following September, Loren Mead noted that the children's group "had operated fitfully, sometimes with good effect, sometimes rather inadequately." After submitting a questionnaire to children and parents, the group developed some new children's programs. The worship group, as Mead reported, "began, floundered a bit, then took hold and really began to carry responsibility for the congregation's life of worship." The consultants had agreed to consult with the task forces, but were unable to visit for this purpose until mid-November. Several telephone calls between Ross and the consultants testified to the frustrations engendered by this time-gap. During one of these calls, Bob Ross told Charlie Winters that he felt "under-employed."

Donovan and Winters visited Birmingham November 18 to 20. After consulting with each of the task forces, they attended a trustees' meeting at which feelings ran high. The trustees, in their letter, had tried to push for their own relationship with the consultants, and now they protested what they saw as "Bob's refusal to let the board of trustees unload in front of Herb and Charlie." "He refused to leave." "It was said to Herb, Charlie, and Bob, 'We're sorry you didn't hear us.' Charlie said, 'We made a mistake. Let's get unloaded.'" The whole issue of the vicar's role now was opened. People remembered the evening as "painful" and "excruciating." They were reluctant to hurt Bob's feelings. At first people said that they trusted him to define his own job, that they didn't know what he was supposed to be doing. Bob Ross gave the following account:

. . . we made a list of functions, with me making most of the inputs. It began to look as if fear of hurting my feelings was well-grounded. I got defensive and they got nervous. Finally Herb and Charlie resorted to extreme measures. They suggested that I go into the next room and listen while the trustees continued to discuss the subject as if I were not present.

This was a device which, though seemingly artificial, freed the trustees so that they could say what was on their minds. It became clear that they felt I was often doing too much and getting in their way, and they also felt jangled by my anxieties about the congregation and my own work in it.

When it was over I was invited back in to give my response to what had been going on. I felt elated! I said, "You know, I think that I could do what you need of me in three days a week, and that is precisely the percentage of my salary you are paying."

In his paper, "The Budgeting of Time," he described the freedom this insight brought him: to get other part-time work, to concentrate on the important functions of his ministry, and to *own* spare time to play and even to volunteer. "Hurrah for the ministry of the laity, because I can get a slice of that action now myself!"

It was a freeing insight for the mission, too. Now they were, in effect, self-supporting, liberated from the onerous burden of a dependent status. It was quite clear that Donovan and Winters had made an important contribution to the Church of the Transfiguration in preparing the way for this part-time contract.

The consultants, the vicar, and the mission continued to work on the question of Ross's role during Winters' and Donovan's visit to Birmingham January 13 to 15. A community meeting was held, at which they dealt with "the question of negotiating the vicar's time and his relationship with the mission as a kind of 'consultant.'" Worship was the area in which Ross's consultant role was most clearly defined. According to Mead, "this proved most satisfactory and functional to the minister and to the first worship group with whom he negotiated the relationship. There was some evidence that later worship groups were not as clear on the role." The first worship group had contracted with the vicar as its consultant. The second group assumed the contract but did not actually renegotiate it. When the third worship group was established, the vicar still assumed the contract, but by then the group had drifted away from this understanding. There were also indications that the role of consultant was a difficult one for Bob Ross to stay within. Some people felt it was good for the development of lay leadership to have Ross acting as a consultant, but others saw an unwillingness to "back off" on his part, a "need to be needed" which could not be met within the consultant role.

Still another facet of the vicar's role had been affected by the work with Donovan and Winters. As a result of data on reactions of neighboring clergy gathered by the consultants and presented to Ross and mission members, Bob Ross had made efforts to improve relations with these other clergy. The mission became less isolated and distrustful as a result of its efforts toward better public relations, and Ross reported in May:

The consequences of all this have been twofold: First, in developing a new acceptance of us, other congregations have begun to change their attitudes about the structure of congregational life. That is to say that they have become more people-oriented and less structure-oriented. Second, we have been subtly changed ourselves as a result of this interfacing and have become more aware of the value and impact of tradition, carried by these other congregations, as a factor in our own lives. Herb and Charlie, on their own initiative, added a great deal to this. The overall result is that Transfiguration has been considerably enhanced and expanded in its viewpoint. In a nutshell, we have become more the Church by interaction with the rest of the Church.

Part of this interaction was taking the form of social action on the part of individual members who worked at the "Crisis Center," and in other action programs. Transfiguration was beginning to be seen as a "training" church, whose members were available for leadership roles in other parishes.

## TERMINATING THE CONSULTATION

The consultants made plans to hold a final meeting at Transfiguration in February. Herb Donovan, who had already gone to a new parish in Newark, New Jersey, felt it was impossible for him to continue with the consultation. Winters was willing to remain available to the mission but was not eager to do so because of the travel involved.

Several Transfiguration people had asked for a chance to talk with the consultants alone without the vicar present. Winters and Donovan arrived in Birmingham on February 26 in time to make such meetings possible, but only one person came to see them. The consultants spent the next morning and afternoon with mission members and vicar to examine the question, "What has happened in Transfiguration during the PTP relationship—good, bad, or indifferent?" Some of the answers were: "shift in responsibility mainly from Bob to the congregation," "clarification of Bob's time," "clarification of money problems," "increase in feeling of security with the diocese," "greater stake or sense of ownership of worship," "children more involved," "clarification of congregation and lab viewpoints in mission," "new faces participating," "less nonproductive self-criticism." An evaluation of the consultative process produced comments about the difficulties caused by geographical distance and the fact that the vicar had selected the people for data-gathering interviews. It was remarked that "the presence of consultants forced a group to address problems responsibly and not to 'bitch'."

Winters and Donovan "could detect no strong with-
drawal pains on the part of the clients," who, following
the termination meeting, kept asking for a "final report."
It would seem that termination, in fact, had not been
achieved at this point.

In May, Loren Mead, with the Rev. James D. Anderson,
assistant to the Bishop of the Diocese of Washington for
Parish Development, held a retrieval-debriefing session
with Donovan and Winters in Washington. The consultants described their work in Birmingham as primarily
"diagnostic." They felt their most important contribution
had been organizing and analyzing the data, and presenting it to the members and vicar. The consultants expressed
their concern that the intellectual quickness and forceful-
ness of the vicar "might sometimes leave others behind
—and as a matter of fact, sometimes the minister might
make intellectual appropriations that were beyond his
emotional appropriations . . . . His personal stamp is
heavy on the congregation."

The retrieval-debriefing report notes the heavy strain on
the consultants caused by long hours of travel, and con-
cludes with the decision that a data-gathering session
ought to be held in Birmingham to determine whether
changes have indeed been made and maintained.


DECISION SETS OFF EXPLOSION

During the period of the consultation, people at Transfiguration had begun to question the wisdom of making
every decision dependent on the consensus of the whole
community. Consensus, they were beginning to feel, was
often time-consuming and difficult to arrive at, and could
be blocked by anyone who did not agree, or who wanted
to throw a monkey wrench into the wheels of decision-
making. Many actions were now being taken by the small

self-destructing groups, but some decisions still had to be made by the whole Transfiguration community.

Such a decision was made at a community meeting on July 6, 1971, a decision to lend a thousand dollars of Transfiguration's eighteen-hundred-dollar savings to provide bail for a member of the Alabama Black Liberation Front who had been in the county jail for a year awaiting trial. A decision was made, by consensus, to vote on the issue, with a two-thirds majority required to pass it.

There were strong feelings on the part of many members of the community that Bob Ross had railroaded through the bail-bond decision. "We can't find a way to decide anything," said one. "We try to be a consensus group, but when the method gets in the way of Bob's getting something done, the consensus gets put aside. Bob decides what he wants to do." Another reported that the vicar presided, even though there was a chairman. There was a feeling that the vicar had applied extra pressure by saying that while the money in question was to pay his salary, he was willing to risk it. Those who were not in favor of putting up the bond money had the impression that their position made them "white racists" in the eyes of the majority. The mission was split, with a bitter minority feeling that "the aggressive people get what they want." A few felt that the "money in a nest egg that people worked hard for was spent for no good purpose." The basic anger, however, was not about the decision itself, but about the way it seemed to have been pushed through with little or no effort to deal with the minority group.

## LEARNINGS FROM THE CONSULTATION

Anger about the bail bond issue was still bubbling when Loren Mead, with the Rev. H. M. Morse, Jr., rector of St. Peter's Church, Oxford, Mississippi, as his teammate,

came to Birmingham in September to try to determine
what changes had occurred at Tranfiguration as a result
of the consultants' work. Mead had the impression of
"loaded-up people," full of the pressure of intense feelings.
Morse saw "a lot of closeness and warmth and heated
bitterness," during the interviews with Transfiguration
people.

A summary of the data from the retrieval conference,
and of the consultation as a whole, brings to light two
kinds of learnings: those emerging from the inner dynamics of the mission's life, and those gleaned from the
consultative process.

## LEARNINGS FROM THE MISSION'S LIFE

### 1 POWER

"Who makes decisions? Who is in charge? Who calls the
shots? How is power shared? How does the minister let
go of power and how do members of the congregation
take it on? Who gets blamed when decisions go wrong?"
With these questions, Mead summarized the mission's
most thorny issue. It had not been possible to raise any
of these questions before the consultation, although both
the vicar and members of the mission had been conscious
that there were problems. The words used about the seat
and exercise of power were very different from the realities. Said one member, "Prior to PTP it was Bob's church
. . . . It was ad hoc, which means he makes the rules and
calls the shots." (It is interesting to note here that the lack
of definite decision-making bodies can be used to obscure
the realities of the exercise of power.)

Some members saw the coming of the consultants as a
way to open up and deal with the power issue, but it was
a long time before it became possible for this loaded question to be raised. People agreed that any changes which

had taken place in the vicar's definition and exercise of his role had been expedited by the consultants. "I think the change in Bob's behavior was due to Herb and Charlie. They asked us if we wanted to have it as Bob's thing." "The destructive thing was Bob's anxiety. Defining Bob's job was a creative kind of thing."

Many people agreed that during the period of the consultation there had been a movement of power away from Bob Ross and toward the board of trustees. "The change I see is a willingness to sit back and let others get in," said one. "He is not jamming things down people's throats." Ross himself says, "I became much less directly involved in the decision-making process . . . ." But, probably because of what was seen as the bail-bond railroading incident, there was uncertainty about whether this transfer of power could be continued and sustained. One member said, "Bob hasn't backed off one bit." Another: "I think Bob is feeling at times that he is not needed. I had to tell him to back off."

Decisions, conflict, communications—problems in all of these areas were involved in the power issue. The consultants had struggled to raise questions with the mission about its decision-making system, and some people had been listening to them. Said one member, "People capitulate in consensus and don't get their feelings out." But the experiment with new methods of decision-making during the bail-bond incident had resulted in division and "conflict without conflict-management," as Mead put it.

The anger about that decision resulted in anger toward Ross, although the members of the mission had reached consensus on their method of making the decision. Mead shared with the congregation his observations that their difficulty in managing their feelings about power and leadership made decision-making extremely difficult. This also had the effect of displacing angry feelings on to their minister whenever unpopular decisions were made, no matter *how* they got made. "I am not as pleased with decision-making now as I was then," said one member. The Church of the Transfiguration needed to do a lot more work in this whole complex area. But at least it was possible to talk about it now. "Everything was shoved under the table before," remembered one parishioner.

From the complex web of issues and problems spun around the exercise of power at Transfiguration, several learnings emerge. The story emphasizes *the importance of the realities of power in a congregation's life, the necessity of becoming aware of those realities, and the difficulty and pain involved in facing them.* With the consultants' help, both vicar and members were able to live through some of this difficulty and pain and arrive at the consultation's most important result—the redefining of Bob Ross's role.

*To the extent that the realities of power are not clearly defined, the process of decision-making is hazardous.* Reactions may take place which are not really reactions to the decision, but reactions to the unclear power issues.

The story of Transfiguration also illustrates that *to the extent that power is shared with the congregation, the sense of ownership of the members is enhanced.* Mission members feel ambivalent about the degree to which the vicar has been able to back off from his leadership role; but it is clear that the worship group, at any rate, has taken on real responsibility and experienced ownership in the area of its concern.

## 2 THE ENVIRONMENT

The Church of the Transfiguration is affected by a peculiar kind of environment. No surrounding ghettos, norms drawn from secular surroundings, or troubled history determined the events in its life. But the ecclesiastical setting of the mission had a powerful effect on its goals, its problems, and its struggles. The story of Transfiguration illustrates the way *judicatory structures and surrounding churches place pressures on a small church to be successful in traditional ways*, affecting its concern for growth, finances, and even its continued existence. The process of consultation made clear that these concerns were not the vital, functional, special concerns of this mission, even though the ecclesiastical environment had been successful in influencing the church to accept them. The story also underlines the way in which *innovation produces alienation and requires courage and support to be sustained.* In spite of some abrasive personal factors which may have obscured and complicated the relationship between Transfiguration and its ecclesiastical environment, these clear learnings were absorbed by consultants, vicar, and members, and the implicit problems were met by some very creative understanding and action.

Another unique feature of Transfiguration's environment was a less external kind of ambiance—the style of the people who were attracted to the experiment and the intensity of the relationships they formed with each other. In a sense, these factors produced a kind of anti-environment, which one member symbolized as "people holding hands facing inward." Every parish experiences the tension between facing inward and facing outward, and has its special ways of living in the paradox created by these opposing demands. At Transfiguration the tension found expression in an explosion created by an attempt to force the church to focus on the external world. *Every parish interacts with its environment, but for each congregation "environment" needs to be described and interpreted in relevant ways.*

LEARNINGS FROM THE CONSULTATIVE PROCESS

1 WHO WAS THE CLIENT?

The problems resulting from uncertainty about the identity of the client were mentioned during the retrieval weekend. Reflecting on that weekend with his parishioners, Bob Ross wrote, "The way our PTP consultation developed, I seemed to become the primary client. This may have been what was needed, I don't know. It meant that I got a lot of attention, that my problems received primary notice, and finally that I learned a lot and made many changes in the way I operated." Looking forward to the possibility of further consultative help, which Mead recommended, Ross said emphatically, "I just need *not* to be the primary client." In this consultation, the vicar was the primary client, but the lack of clarity about this fact produced confusion and anger among the members. The fact that a shifting ad hoc committee negotiated the contract compounded the confusion. *Consultants and congregations can avoid a lot of problems when the identity of the client is clear.*

2 THE IMPORTANCE OF CONTRACTS

The most satisfactory result of the consultants' work at Transfiguration was the clarification of expectations of the vicar and the renegotiation of his role. The story also illustrates the value of contracts as a part of the necessary ongoing support system for task forces.

3 GEOGRAPHICAL AND TRAVEL PROBLEMS

These problems, which had been so difficult for the consultants, were also noted by Transfiguration people, one of whom said, "Their schedule was terrible. They had to be married to a clock." At one point, because of their schedule, the only way the consultants could be in touch was through a conference call from Houston. Perhaps the learning here is that long distances between consultant and congregation, and the resultant schedule difficulties, can produce a lot of frustration.

### 4 THE CONSULTANTS' ROLE

The consultants' view of their work as primarily diagnostic seemed to have been shared by mission members, whose most vivid memory of the consultation was of the data presentation. This had been a shocking experience, provoking reactions of disbelief and anger, but also producing important changes in the mission's life. "They helped us see crises as problems that can be worked on and solved." Mead and Morse identified the work on Ross's contractual relationship to the congregation and to the worship group as the contribution most clearly identified as helpful by the mission. It was interesting that the Donovan-Winters reports had not emphasized this accomplishment of the consultation. Members of the mission sensed complementary roles in the consultant team, Winters providing support and encouragement, Donovan providing analytical and managerial skills, although the consultants did not plan or intend such a distinction.

The Transfiguration experience clearly demonstrates *the value of a third-party consultant in clarifying and enhancing the relationship between a clergyman and a congregation, and the powerful effect of data presentation in that work.*

### 5 TERMINATION

Arrangements for the retrieval conference seemed to indicate, once more, that the consultation had not been successfully terminated. In a quarterly report, it was recorded that, "Approval was given for Bob to contact Loren Mead asking him to come during our September re-grouping period to help us look at ourselves, clarify our goals, and organize for the future." This sounds rather more like a plan to begin a new consultation than to evaluate a consultation recently concluded. Mead noted in advance of the weekend his "uncertainty about my role in Birmingham when I visit on September 9 to 12—in view of the 'pressure' I'm feeling from Ross." When Mead spoke to the mission during the visit, he clarified the primary purpose of his visit—to gather information for PTP, but he also presented a report on the consultation and some impressions of the issues at Transfiguration which might well "help them to look at themselves." These contradictory expectations highlight the fact that *termination of a consultation has not necessarily been accomplished because it has been announced.*

CONCLUSION

During the retrieval interviews, one Transfiguration member looked forward: "I think the future is good because we have survived. This is the kind of church we have been looking for. We have a lot of work to do." The story of the Church of the Transfiguration is an important story because it shows how a young mission was enabled to live into its future with a new clarity about the issues in its life. It can also be an important story for the rich learnings about parish dynamics and the consultative process which might contribute to the futures of other congregations.

Celia A. Hahn

# 7

## LEARNINGS ABOUT CONGREGATIONS
## IN CHANGE

Besides the specific learnings at the end of each congregation's story, there are a number of broader learnings that run through all of the chapters. None of these observations are by any means definitive answers; but they are indicative of the very nature of parish life, and are descriptions rather than prescriptions. Since they describe a process, not a program, they are not meant to be copied. The following learnings are offered as ideas about how parishes operate and how change can take place. It is hoped that these ideas, shown concretely through parish stories, will help the reader learn more about his own parish.

(1) *Commitment and Investment* in congregations is enormous. Each of these six cases shows a group of people who freely give an extraordinary amount of time, attention, and energy to their parish. Busy men and women spend hours of their time at night meetings, all-day workshops on Saturday, and weekend retreats. At All Souls, Richmond, one committee described "forty meetings, ten hours each" just to analyze data from the congregational

meeting. At Dumbarton Church in Washington, individuals serve on several committees that meet weekly or on Saturdays. Parish work and Sunday church attendance are taken for granted and have become a natural way of life. Consultation often adds a demand for more of the parishioners' time and energy.

Commitment is not only a matter of time but also of emotional investment. During data-gathering interviews with parishioners, people became very emotional while telling their parish story, sometimes to the point of tears as they spoke of painful memories. Some of the pain took the form of grief over people or things that had changed or been lost in some way. There was grief over a lost charter in the Pee Dee and sorrow over a pastor's leaving in Chicago. Members of Transfiguration, Birmingham, described a meeting as "painful" or "excruciating." There were also deep feelings of anger over unresolved conflict. Several members of Dumbarton were angry and highly frustrated over their church's social action policies, yet they continued to participate in parish work. In 1967 the merger of two Chicago congregations resulted in such strong feelings that even today some members still continue to defend "their version" of the merger story.

Personal emotional investment is shown with joy and pride as well as pain. The parishioner who told his bishop that he ought to move his cathedral to the missions of the Pee Dee spoke out of that celebrative pride. When the vicar of Transfiguration, Birmingham, wrote "Hurray for the ministry of the laity . . ." he reflected joy in something new he had discovered in his own life and in his congregation.

People belong to congregations because they want to. No one has to join. James Anderson,* suggests that peo-

---

* James Anderson, the author of *To Come Alive* (Harper and Row, 1973).

ple come to church not to join, but to be healed. The kind of commitment in these congregations suggests that Anderson is right, and that the people of these six congregations have very deep investments in finding health and wholeness through their local church.

(2) A *Parish's History* is a powerful influence on its present life. Parishes, like people, have a past. The present style of each congregation comes from the events and people that went before it. Each parish is molded by its history. Dumbarton's congregation has appealed to many younger people with modern outlooks yet the congregation remembers its historical past, is very much in touch with its tradition, and uses the traditional biblical and liturgical words of the Christian faith. At the Church of the Pee Dee, each individual chapel had to overcome a long history of competition in order to work together. Historically each chapel had been jealous and suspicious of the other. When they realized that they would die apart, the four really made history when they began to work together.

(3) A *Parish's Environment* is an important factor in its life. Each congregation has a specific geography and social climate which influence its life and need to be considered when working for change. Environment means different things to different people.

For St. Paul and The Redeemer, its geography has a profound impact upon everything the congregation does. The church is situated in an interracial, middle-class island in the south side of Chicago. The doors of the church have to be locked because of the community's problem with crime. Although individual members and the rector are involved in social outreach, the church as a corporate entity does not reach out to the ghetto, a reflection of the neighborhood's isolation from its surroundings.

In Texarkana, the element of environment that seems most influential for St. James is the pattern of behavior within the community. These patterns directly influence who goes to what meetings in the parish and who influences decisions. Although the congregation is one place that is seen as trying to operate across class and social barriers, it remains difficult to overcome these influences and standards.

At the Church of the Transfiguration, Birmingham, the psychological environment was more determinative than the physical. An emphasis on innovation and personal growth characterizes Transfiguration's experimental style.

(4) *Tension Between Commitment to Outward Concerns and/or Inward Concerns* can be a source of growth for the parish. Parishes are aware of the biblical command to go out into all the world and proclaim the good news. This outward thrust is Christian witnessing by word and action. Another aspect of Christian witness is to take care of one's own flock, to nurture the people and to build them up in the faith. In these six stories, the parishes are continually pulled between these two directions. Each one works out the tension in its own way.

In Chicago, St. Paul and The Redeemer has chosen to emphasize spiritual and personal growth on a corporate parish level. As individuals they move out into the community and are very active in civic and neighborhood affairs.

In Texarkana, St. James opens up its facilities to the community and allows the rector to carry out a very active social ministry. The congregation is corporately more inward oriented than outward oriented.

In Washington, Dumbarton is constantly experiencing

the tension of conflicting commitments. This tension has provided an opportunity to clarify the parish's identity and come to some consensus. The congregation is committed to both social action and personal growth, though the latter has a higher priority. Dumbarton is always working at balancing these two directions.

(5) *There Are a Variety of Styles of Consultative Help.* Just as no two churches are alike, no two consultants or consultant teams are alike. Each story in this book describes a distinct approach to consultation. In three cases teams of consultants were used. Al Persons and Mac Willson, from their experience at St. James, Texarkana, clearly show that it was important to them to keep in touch with each other, paying attention to the way they worked together. Consultant team members often complement each other in style. Transfiguration members saw their consultants in very different ways. Winters provided support and encouragement, while Donovan provided analytical and managerial skills. Persons and Willson, as priest and layman, were also seen to have complementary roles and skills. Each consultant or team brings its own flavor and personality to the consultation.

Three of the six consultations were carried out by a one-man effort. Herb Gravely, Irving Stubbs, and Larry Ulrich all worked independently, although Herb Gravely's wife, Mary Jeane, often acted as an observer, giving an outside perspective to his consultation. Another approach is that of Irving Stubbs. He is a full-time professional consultant with his own firm, TRUST, Inc., which had a contract with the Hanover Presbytery to provide consultative assistance to parishes. Through that contract the presbytery provided financial support for the work at All Souls.

(6) *Parish Information Is Powerful.* One of the major tasks of a consultant is to help the congregation find out what it needs to know in order to make decisions more responsibly and effectively. The consultant also helps the congregation learn how to deal with issues that arise long after the consultant has completed his contract. In many ways, what the consultant does is help the congregation hold up a mirror to see its own life more clearly. In each of the six cases in this book it was difficult for the parish to assimilate the information, whether it was developed by a consultant or a parish group. Often the material was seen to be threatening, and the experience of looking at the information was always powerful and challenging.

In Birmingham at Transfiguration Church, when Donovan and Winters reported to the congregation what they had learned in extended interviews from members, there were strong feelings—some of disbelief, some of shock, some of support. The event, however, led to important changes in the mission's life.

At All Souls, Richmond, members gathered for an all-day congregational meeting. They heard a statement of identity and also had an opportunity to give their own input. This turned out to be one of the most crucial events for All Souls' change efforts.

The power of information about parishes was reaffirmed in events occurring during the research and writing of this book. A rough draft of each chapter was shared with the parish and the consultants for their comments and factual corrections. In each case, the rereading of their story was difficult for parish members, sometimes bringing to their attention dimensions they did not know about personally. Immediate reactions were strong, and in several cases further visits to the congregation were needed to help work through the material. In itself, having a case history written proved to be a powerful intervention in the life of the parishes. In all six cases, however, that intervention was seized as an opportunity for further growth.

(7) *Parish Norms Are Difficult to Change.* Every parish builds up habitual ways of doing things over the course of its history. These norms are usually unwritten codes that describe "how we do things around here." They are so taken for granted that no one thinks to talk about them. Parish norms are seen in the way people behave and in the way they dress for parish or vestry meetings, the way decisions get made, the way money troubles are handled, and the way differences of opinion are dealt with.

These informal patterns of behavior mold the climate of a congregation's life and contribute to a parish's unique identity. While it is relatively easy to change surface events in a congregation, these deep-lying norms are extremely difficult to change. They require careful attention and inputs of energy over a considerable period of time. Indeed, many congregations become frustrated because surface changes do not continue to hold up if underlying norms are not changed. People also tend to underestimate the difficulty of achieving deep-level change, thinking that surface change is all that is needed.

Both Richard Allen at St. James, Texarkana, and Warner White at St. Paul and The Redeemer, Chicago, made a self-conscious attempt to modify their style of leadership to allow greater involvement of members. This led to a change in the rector's pattern of having all the authority, responsibility, and leadership. Both St. James' and St. Paul and The Redeemer's efforts were long-term and required great strength to sustain. Their own previous patterns and the expectations of the congregations put pressure on them to revert to earlier styles of leadership. They were helped by supportive lay people, the coaching and support of the consultants, and by their own willingness to cooperate.

The situation at Dumbarton is ambiguous, but that ambiguity points up another learning. While the consultation was in progress and the consultant on the job, there was a strong feeling that the parish had changed a norm. Previously, conflict had tended to break people into polarized camps, but during the consultation differences were dealt with without leading to polarization. Members also felt they had learned to be more responsive to each other. Now that some time has passed since the consultation has been terminated, some members of the congregation are unsure that the change was a lasting one.

It takes great effort to institute change on the normative level, and it takes sustained effort over a period of time to build new norms into the life of the congregation. There are many temptations and pressures to revert to previous behavior. Lasting change only occurs when the new norms become the accustomed pattern.

(8) *Previous Learnings by Project Test Pattern* have been reinforced. Loren Mead, in PTP's first book, *New Hope for Congregations*, identified specific learnings about parish life and the processes of change. Those learnings were developed from the four case histories in that book and are also verified by the six case histories in *Congregations in Change*.

Earlier learnings about parishes include the ideas that congregations can change, that they have history, that they are unique, and that they are corporate, interpersonal systems. These six cases in *Congregations in Change* reaffirm those learnings, some of which can now be expanded. The new learnings about the difficulty of changing parish norms reinforce and point to Mead's learning that parishes are complex systems.

In *New Hope for Congregations*, Mead also identified five learnings directly related to the process of change in a parish: that third party consultation assists change; that contracts or covenants can help change to happen; that the clergyman is a key to change; that support systems are important; and that failure itself can produce significant learning. *Congregations in Change* shows a variety of consultant styles. These cases also point out the importance of a clear contract between the consultant and the client parish. When the congregation begins to change and grow, then the clergyman often becomes more effective in his own role. As parish leaders take more initiative and responsibility for the parish life, and as parishioners support the changes, then the pastor often develops new capacities to risk, to collaborate; and he becomes more creative in his relationship with others.

Two other former PTP learnings are seen in *Congregations in Change*. The Diocese of South Carolina's supportive relationship to the Church of the Pee Dee reaffirms the importance of judicatory support for change efforts on a local level. Dumbarton church's story and All Souls' story also support this idea. The final learning of the earlier volume was that valuable learnings can come from failure. Indeed, these six cases show that a parish's willingness to risk failure is a prime indicator of its ability to change.

6580